Michiel Stofferis grew up in a rural part of The Netherlands. With a passion for geology, he pursued a career in the oil industry but always wondered why people hardly recognise the strong link between increased hydrocarbon use, growing affluence and consequent rising world population. Michiel has been influenced by environmental writers and has a keen interest in planetary sustainability, inequality and the evolution of mankind through the ages. Currently he is concerned about how people deal with moral dilemmas and fairness.

Dedication

To my wife, Anneli Nilsson

Michiel Stofferis

A HOLISTIC TREATISE ON OVERPOPULATION

AUSTIN MACAULEY PUBLISHERS™

LONDON · CAMBRIDGE · NEW YORK · SHARJAH

A CIP catalogue record for this title is available from the British Library.

ISBN 9781788482127 (Paperback)
ISBN 9781788482134 (Hardback)
ISBN 9781788482141 (E-Book)

www.austinmacauley.com

First Published (2018)
Austin Macauley Publishers Ltd™
25 Canada Square
Canary Wharf
London
E14 5LQ

Acknowledgements

I would like to acknowledge Carl Lee (Sheffield University) and Jonathon Porritt (Forum for the Future) for reading the first drafts of the book and providing me with constructive comments.

Preface

I will probably be metaphorically mauled for writing a book on overpopulation. To advocate a smaller number of children per couple is seen by most of us as an intrusion in one's personal life or the life of one's family. The number of children one has is considered sacrosanct and grounded in rights and laws. However, due to globalisation and the internet, the world and our common human culture are evolving rapidly. Thus, we are now less tolerant to excesses happening within the shrouded protection of a family, such as abuse, suppression of women's rights or FGM. What happens within family limits can stay no longer sacrosanct in a world which is increasingly connected and dependent on each other.

A closer look at rights reveals that human beings have the right to procreate, but we do not have the right to procreate without any limits. We need to take consideration of others as well. Specifically, the United Nations' World Population Plan of Action mentions that people exercising this right should *"take into account the needs of their living and future children, and their responsibilities toward the community."*[1]

The freedom to do whatever we want diminishes with more people around us. Playing loud music in a barn in the middle of nowhere does not bother anybody. But, when one is surrounded by hundreds of other people, playing loud music becomes a nuisance. We have anti-smoking laws to protect others from passive smoking. But if cities become so big, that we need to sit in a car for 2 hours to cover 10 km, pack ourselves in an overcrowded train or breathe heavily polluted air, is that

---

[1] WPPA, para 14(f) in Principles and Objectives

something we just need to endure? Just like passive smoking, should we not start to look at the root causes?

The concept of overpopulation is relatively new. Malthus in the late 18th century, Paul Ehrlich and the report for the Club of Rome in the 1960s and 1970s, have highlighted an existential threat to our species. The realisation of limits on food production and essential resources were not considered to be compatible with an ever-increasing human population. However, Malthus' worries were alleviated by the wonders of the Industrial Revolution, whilst Ehrlich and the Report for the Club of Rome wrote their worries without fully understanding the profound impact on crop yield by using fertilisers at industrial-scale (Green Revolution).

But concerns about these limits have not gone away fully. If we take the current inequality in the world for granted, the immediate concern of an increasing population may not be the limits on food production or resources. But is it fair to maintain the status quo between rich developed countries and the developing world? With the current technological progress, it is impossible that everybody on the planet can lead a life like an American, certainly not when the population is still growing. Or do we want to accept lower living standards in the developed world to accommodate a reasonable life for everybody? That seems unlikely.

On top of this, we now realise that there are also ecological limitations, such as the loss of biodiversity and global warming, which threaten our existence indirectly. Global warming, resulting from increasing atmospheric CO_2 concentrations, will cause a rise in sea levels and will drive climatic change. The rise in atmospheric CO_2 is caused by burning more and more fossil fuels, which in turn is caused both by increases in affluence (higher energy use) and population growth. Rising sea levels and climatic change will have an influence on the amount of arable land, threaten coastal cities or reduce crop yield due to droughts, temperature rises or too much rain in other areas. These could consequently drive mass migration, which in some areas is already happening.

By highlighting the innovative traits of our species and its rapid developments, existential worries are often dismissed by the technocratic elite and their influential press by bolstering statements, such as: *"Look what we have achieved so far!" "Why worry? Just like in the past we will find another solution!" "Look what the Internet has brought us!" "We will replace fossil fuels by solar"*. I do not want to debate that certain future innovations will be feasible, but at the same time it should be realised that within a historical perspective, innovations come in spurts and not in a continuous line. And does an optimistic outlook for the future warrant a carte blanche for unlimited population growth? There are other concerns than atmospheric CO_2 content. Continuous population growth will continue the sprawling of cities, roads, arable land and mines and will cause havoc on the environment.

As much as we are concerned on the impact of the planetary limits of food and resources, we also are beginning to realise that the environment we live in is in a poor state. More species have become extinct than ever before. Even though biodiversity is important to us, we rely increasingly on GM foods, fertilisers and pesticides for our large-scale food production. It is a fragile equilibrium and there is no way back to the past. Woods, mountains and open grasslands are also important for our own relaxation and well-being. Of course, as a social species we are empathic towards each other, but many wild species get our sympathy too and we feel sad when their numbers dwindle. The planet has a limited carrying capacity for humans and certainly for humans with a high energy and resource consumption.

The increasing world population is driven by a large family size and a rapid increase of life expectancy. Family size has often a cultural background such as patriarchy, teenage marriage and entitlements to polygamy. Large families are more prone to abuse, demand extraordinary parental efforts and cause insufficient development of their children; and, since large families start early, young parents miss out on their own development in life. The negative effects of a large family size are exacerbated by the fact that more and more people are flocking to cities in search of a better existence but where it is near impossible to maintain a large family size. In cities, children with many siblings often end up on the streets, prone to abuse and exploitation. Rising inequality is in parts related to a rapidly increasing world population causing more unemployment and misery in the developing world which could lead to migration on a large scale.

Increased life expectancy is a result of better hygiene, medical progress and better care. With the rapid rise of the old age cohort, legitimate questions can be raised on the affordability of a long life after working. Although a declining fertility rate will shrink the world population, a too rapid decline risks that the population pyramid will become top-heavy and unsustainable in this transition period. With insufficient pensions to provide for old age, people will need to work longer or they might be destined to poverty again. The quality of life of old age is important and the related costs should take priority over medical research costs to extend life even further.

An increasing world population will reduce our quality of life in general. Traffic jams, queues in shops, noise of neighbours or from trains, cars or planes are increasingly already part of our life. It affects our health whilst we are shoehorned into subsistence jobs because of increasing competition and ongoing automation. The resulting migration is causing troubles for others. Sharing with others is a very human trait, but sharing unconditionally is not. So, if one's quality of life is going downhill, there comes a point where we do not want to share anymore and borders and doors will shut.

Overpopulation due to large family sizes can be avoided by contraceptive methods. A large part of the world population is already reducing its family size, largely driven by economic reasons. But if others do not want to take responsibility and procreate without limits and implicitly hope that the extended family, the tribe, society in general or neighbouring countries will act as a relieve valve for their excess of children, then this will create an unnecessary strain. Human societies, the environment and the world as a whole are thus tested to their limits.

It is time to take family size seriously and develop a framework of legislation. This should start in the developed world, where there is less cultural bias towards smaller families and where legislation on similar issues (e.g. gender equality, rights of homosexuals) is already well accepted. The developed nations can thus act as a role model for developing nations. I would propose to use financial disincentives to regulate the family size to a maximum of two children per couple. This could come in the form of a progressive tax on parents who want more than two children. Such a child-tax should also be progressive on income to prevent celebrity chefs, politicians or pop stars showing off with large trophy families and thus sending out the wrong messages of envy to the less fortunate. Some people feel that limiting to two children per couple is not enough to quickly curb the world population. Although the developed nations with their higher energy consumption probably need to limit their size even more, I think it will already be difficult enough, due to cultural or religious bias, to achieve a two-child limit for everyone in the world.

In the developing world, we should bring living conditions and GDP in line with the developed nations. It is realised that this will increase the overall need for food, energy and resources, which will have repercussions on the environment of the planet. It is morally just however to help these people out of their misery. The western world is indebted to the developing nations since it has a historical legacy of exploitation during the days of slavery and colonisation. Also, setting up pension funds in developing nations for example will remove worries for old age-care and reduce one of the incentives to have a large family size.

Simultaneously, it is of paramount importance to bring the fertility rate down in the developing world. Education of men and women is essential and frank dialogues need to be held to tackle antiquated cultures and religions, whilst emphasising a common culture in our globalised world. Teenage marriage and polygamy should disappear and made truly illegal in every country in the world. It is important to stress sustainability both for the environment as for the nations themselves. It is not good to take in excess from the environment; it is not good to rely too much on your neighbours for external help; it is not good to use economic migration to other countries as a relieve valve.

Finally, historical experience of the forced abortions in China, forced vasectomies in India and compulsory sterilisations of black women during the days of the Eugenics laws in the US, show that coercion never works. People should be convinced not forced.

Chapter 1
Why a Book on Overpopulation?

Too many of us.

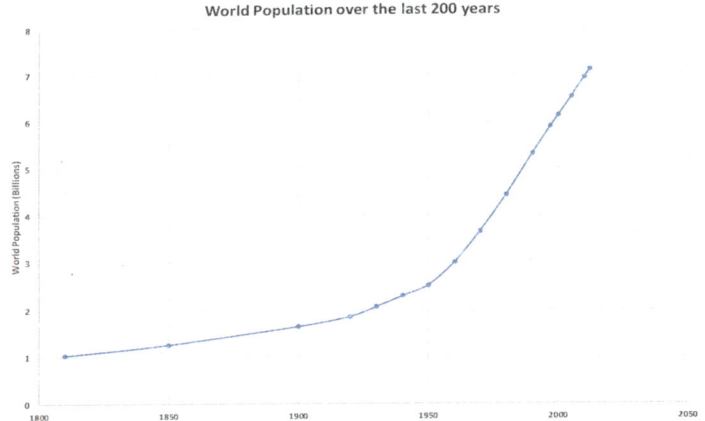

Figure 1-1: World Population Rise since industrial Revolution[2]

I have worked my professional life in the oil and gas industry. It has always puzzled me that the influence of hydrocarbon extractions on our wellbeing and on population growth has been taken for granted. The inventions of the Industrial Revolution and the inexpensive availability and large-scale use of hydrocarbon fuels during the 19th century enabled us to gradually support more and more people. The per capita energy consumption increased

---

[2] Data from http://ourworldindata.org/data/population-growth-vital-statistics/world-population-growth/

steadily from the start of Industrial Revolution onwards (see Figure 1-2) and is due to the increasing use of fossil fuels, first coal and later oil and gas.

Needless to say, not all energy consumption is equally distributed in the world. At the top end, an average US citizen currently consumes annually around 300 GJ[3], whilst some small oil producing countries far exceed this number. At the bottom end, a country like Afghanistan only consumes annually 3.8 GJ per capita.[4] And of course, there are differences within a country with rich people consuming vast amounts more than poorer people: The 500 million richest people on the planet are responsible for half the global CO_2 emissions.[5]

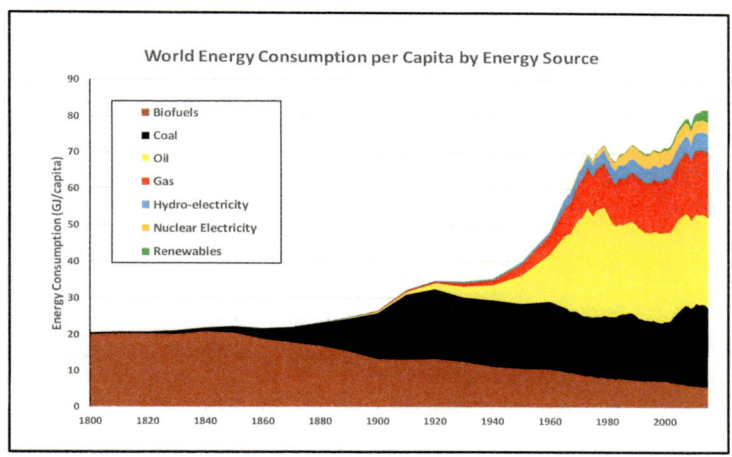

Figure 1-2: Historical per capita annual energy consumption[6]

---

[3] GJ is Giga (one billion) Joule

[4] Energy use per capita – World-bank, December 2012 (via Wikipedia)

[5] *This Changes Everything*. Naomi Klein (2014). Penguin edition 2015 p. 114.

[6] Data pre-1965 from http://ourworldindata.org/ data/resources-energy/energy-production-and-changing-energy-sources/; data post-1965 from http://www.bp.com/en/global/corporate/energy-economics/statistical-review-of-world-energy.html. Biofuel data (wood/plants) were not available from the BP reference and were interpolated and extrapolated from the first reference (ourworldindata). Per capita numbers obtained from world population numbers of ref. 1.

Historical dependency of fossil fuels and population is underestimated. Currently it is impossible to support the existing world population with food and energy, without the use of fossil fuel production. In that respect, it does not make sense to talk about a world population of 7 billion with the energy use per capita of 200 years ago (i.e. 20 GJ/capita). This is only feasible if we are all prepared to live like an average Kenyan or Pakistani (see Figure 1-3). For most of us there is no way back to the past.

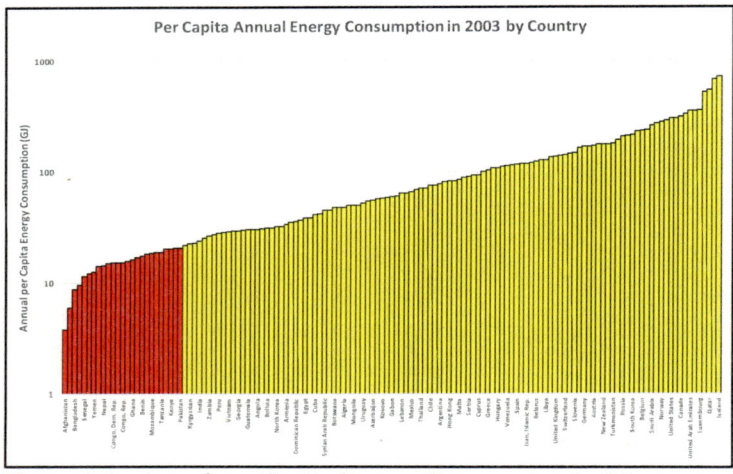

Figure 1-3: Annual per Capita Energy Consumption in GJ (Logarithmic scale) by country in 2003[4]. The countries in red have per capita energy use of pre-industrial times (20 GJ/per capita per year or less). Most countries have 2013 data as well, which are not much different however.

We live in a confined space, called Planet Earth, with limited resources. Initially we thought it was Malthusian food scarcity, but we overcame that by our own inventiveness, by scores of industrial discoveries in the 19th and 20th centuries, by advances in medical science and by a bountiful supply of hydrocarbon based energy. Later in the 20th century, doubts were expressed by the

Report for the Club of Rome Project[7], in which, for the first time, computer projections were used. Their focus was primarily on the limits of (non-renewable) energy resources, minerals, productivity as well as pollution. Their estimates on population proved to be very accurate but projections for resources were over-pessimistic. They failed to see the effects of large-scale use of fertilisers to increase crop yield, the effects of drilling horizontal oil wells on oil reserves or the effects of banning CFC's to prevent the ozone hole of spreading.

Although we have probably enough fossil fuel reserves for a couple of hundred years, we now realise that the limits are not the amount of fossil fuel resources but rather the effects of burning them. A full conversion to renewable energy sources will be gradual and in the meantime, the greenhouse gases in the atmosphere (mainly CO_2 and methane) are reaching dangerous levels to the point that our climate is irreversibly changing. We may have enough land area and the potential to intensify agriculture even further to feed more than 10 billion, but at what costs? The biodiversity of the planet is reducing dramatically by conversion of nature into farmland whilst farm animals' well-being is compromised by even more needed industrial-style farming.

Although I am a lifelong environmentalist, I am struck by the naivety of some people, who claim that agro-ecological methods could be the magic answer to all our food supply problems.[8] I have not seen a convincing study which relies on more than a couple of encouraging experiments, whilst taking into account future climatic changes and feeding a well-balanced diet to more than 10 billion future citizens. Too easily and without much scientific basis, critiques from big agri-businesses or the GM-industry on the current state of agro-ecological methods are immediately waived as governed by self-interest.

The issue of population and its impact on global consumption is sometimes described as the 'elephant in the room' – a problem

---

[7] *The Limits to Growth* – A report for the Club of Rome Project on the Predicament of Mankind. Dennis L. Meadows ea. (1972)

[8] *This Changes Everything*. Naomi Klein (2014) Penguin edition 2015 pp 134-135

that the world ignores as it is politically and ethically difficult to tackle.[9] Population control is not an easy subject and to give ready-made solutions is very difficult. The world is moving forward at different speeds with some remote tribes still practically in the Stone Age, whilst urban western regions are evolving into much different lifestyles.

Population pressure on the environment and CO_2 emissions is often refuted by claiming that the real cause is over-consumption of the rich (countries). Discussion of expanding population numbers as one of other contributing reasons for a deteriorating environment is considered as immoral[10], since this would mostly blame the poorer people.[11] In this book, I would like to break this morality taboo of the impact population has on the environment, by mentioning other reasons to stop population growth. In densely populated areas of the world, our quality of life and health are constantly compromised and more people will make this even worse. The effects of overpopulation on the economy or as a cause of wars and consequent human suffering are underexposed. Large family sizes that also threaten family cohesions, are unlikely to be sustainable in this modern globalised world and are thus causing increased misery for a significant part of mankind.

Before addressing the problems of the developing world, it is necessary to discuss policies for family size combined with a legal framework in the developed nations, which are less stifled by cultural or religious prejudices. The developed nations already provide role models for the emancipation of women, rights for homosexuals or outlawing FGM. To prevent excessive climate change, the world population should shrink. Moreover, only small families can consistently assure a healthy development for each child and do not exhaust parents excessively. A smaller family size, not exceeding two children per couple, is needed for all of

---

[9] http://www.bbc.co.uk/news/science-environment-29788754

[10] *"...the persistent positing of population control as a solution to climate change is a distraction and a moral dead end" This Changes Everything.* Naomi Klein (2014) Penguin edition 2015 pp 114

[11] *How Did We Get into This Mess?* George Monbiot. Verso (2016). Chapter 18

us. The developed world and some of the developing countries are already on this track, albeit mostly by economic necessity.

Based on historical experience, we should shy away from coercive methods. Forced methods are never working longer term and are causing much human suffering. Other types of stimuli are needed than coercion, such as abolishing child benefits as of the third child and introducing a child-tax instead, progressive with the number of children and income. The income dependency is really needed to prevent some of the richer elites considering a large offspring as a privilege. There is no point allowing a large family only for the rich, because they can afford it. This is the same outdated culture of a chief in a polygamous society, maintaining many women. It is time for everybody to have a responsible number of children and to show allegiance across the classes.

I have written this book largely for a post-religious audience in the western world. It is predominantly religion which has been holding back the worldwide use of anti-conception and denying abortion rights for women. Religious fundamentalists seem to prioritise the morality of unborn life rather than the immorality of a sub-human existence. Since only a small (but growing) part of humanity is weaned off religion relatively recently, taboos on capping the number of children persist, since this is considered as private business. I feel, however, that the stranglehold of religion is gradually waning in the world and that focussing on a common culture to combat global problems is a much-needed necessity.

Chapter 2
Causes, Effects and Questions

Background to Population Growth

Population growth has not been stable over the ages and the world population has never been truly constant, since climate change (famines), wars or epidemics caused fluctuations. There are three main periods relevant for population growth, which are strongly linked to human inventions. For a very long period, human beings lived a nomadic existence as hunter-gatherers. Population was roughly constant during this long period and mainly governed by the presence or absence of food, which in turn had its cause in climatic changes or over-hunting.

This period came to an end to most of us with the development of agriculture. Agriculture did not come at the same time for all human beings and to date some non-contacted tribes in remote tropical rainforests continue to live like hunter-gatherers. Agriculture did not come out of the blue and is strongly correlated with the invention of sophisticated stone tools in the Neolithic era. For most of us, agriculture came fast and spread out fast. The first evidence was in Iran more than 12000 years ago, but by around 3000 years ago most of us led an agricultural life.

The main thing agriculture brought us was food security. Gone were the days that there were no more animals left to hunt or that no food was left by the end of winter. The ability to increase food security by domestication of animals (cattle, sheep, goats) or storage of crops (cereals, corn) allowed a much higher population. Refinement of agricultural tools from the Neolithic to the Bronze and Iron ages, made it possible to rely more and more on agriculture and the population could rise even further. In this period, vast tracts of land were cleared for agriculture to support the expanding population and landscapes were changed for ever since. The earth seemed to be able to provide this bounty however and gradually we got used to this land of plenty and ever more. Another feature of changing landscapes was the development of towns and cities. Human beings have a natural tendency to live close together and towns and cities provided an economy of scale, which accelerated this process.

Apart from changing landscapes, agriculture also brought a major change in diet, since people were more relying on staple food. This over-reliance on a few types of crop caused some health issues, since the agricultural diet was less varied compared to the food obtained by hunting or gathering. Although food security increased after the agricultural revolution, the labour time and efforts increased as well, necessitating an increased calorific intake. Food security came at a cost: toiling on the land to till the earth and harvest proved time-consuming and hard in comparison to hunting or picking wild fruits. The development of town and cities in agricultural times also gave rise to epidemics, which raged easier in crowded places with poor sanitation.

Agriculture thus became a blessing but also a curse, since the population increased so substantially, that it was impossible to feed this increased population by only hunting or gathering. As often with human progress, progress is irreversible and there is no way back to the past. Although pre-agricultural times were hard with more frequent famines and low life expectancy, there is a kind of yearning for this lost world. Could this be the meaning of the biblical paradise and John Milton's *Paradise Lost*?

The second milestone in human evolution is the Industrial Revolution (1820–1850). Major inventions (e.g. steam engine, textile machinery) resulted in the start of industry, creating low cost products at a large scale. It also had a strong effect on the development of agriculture. Mechanisation not only increased yields (more could be done in the same time) but also drove millions of people from the hard labour on the land to the hard labour in factories and mines.

In this age of innovation, a string of new discoveries and applications spawned other innovations and improvements with an ever-increasing efficiency. Major medical discoveries in late 19th and early 20th century (understanding of virology, penicillin, large scale use of anaesthetics) as well as the realisation of the importance of hygiene, increased life expectancy dramatically (see Figure 2-1). Another driver for the drop of mortality is the ever-reducing violence. Despite the increase in absolute numbers, victims of wars and conflict (refer to two world wars in the 20th century), violent deaths per capita are decreasing.[12]

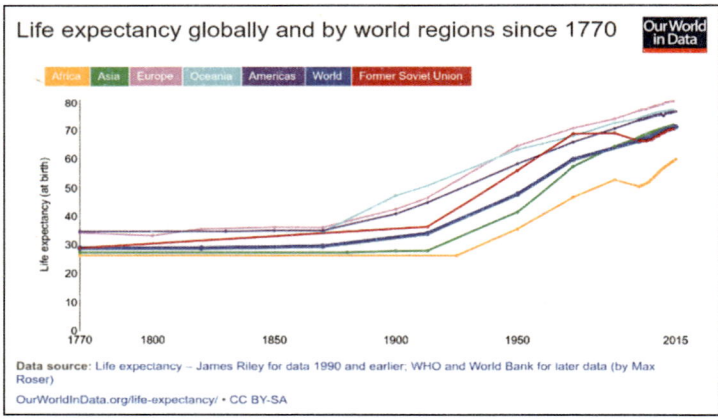

Figure 2-1: Life expectancy soared dramatically from the second half of the 19th century. Note the inequality and catching up of Africa and Asia.[13]

A third milestone, important for population growth is the so-called Green Revolution (1960–1970), which saw massive increases in crop yield per hectare due to large scale use of artificial fertiliser, mechanisation and crop upgrading. The large-scale use of fertiliser was enabled by the cheap availability of methane, the largest component of natural gas, as a hydrogen source and nitrogen from the atmosphere. This is known as the Haber-Bosch process, invented and perfected in the first half of

---

[12] *The Better Angels of Our Nature* – Steven Pinker (2011)

[13] Max Roser (2016) – '*Life Expectancy*'. Published online at OurWorldInData.org. Retrieved from:
https://ourworldindata.org/life-expectancy/

the 20th century, but only used at a large industrial scale as of the 1950s. Note that currently 3–5% of the world's natural gas production is consumed in the Haber-Bosch process.[14]

Previously agricultural soil was fertilised by manure and bird guano, which were limited at the time (no large-scale farming was in place yet and guano deposits were relatively scarce). The use of artificial fertiliser increased the yield per hectare dramatically, which in turn allowed the support of a much bigger population. Particularly in the developing world (India and Africa) the Green Revolution eradicated persistent hunger. With world population ballooning after this technological advance,[15] another irreversible barrier was crossed. At the moment, it is impossible to feed the world population without the massive use of artificial fertiliser and we are reliant on the source (natural gas) and the high-energy requirements to make it. With the world population growing, the use of fertiliser is set to increase (see Figure 2-2).

The rapid successions of improvements and innovations have made mankind overconfident: "Do not worry, we find another solution to our problems." The crossing of barriers of the Agricultural, Industrial and Green Revolutions have made mankind more prosperous but the large associated population growths resulting from these crossings have made us as a species more vulnerable as well. We cannot go back to the past.

---

[14] https://en.wikipedia.org/wiki/Haber_process

[15] Some authors feel that the Green Revolution caused the fertility rate to drop, see *Peoplequake* by Fred Pearce (2011) Eden Project books, p.89. Pearce reasons that less people are needed to work the land and that people therefore had less children. The big spurt in population growth after the start of the Green Revolution is evidence of the contrary. Indirectly it is true that with less agricultural needs, people were moving to cities to make a living. The absence of an extended family and more expensive housing in cities caused the fertility rate to drop. It can be argued however that the migration into cities would have happened anyway, when rural areas were unable to feed its booming population.

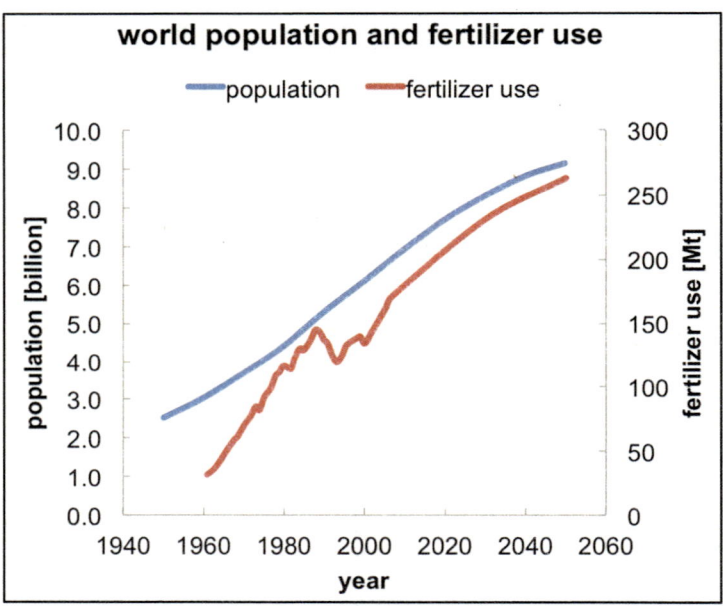

Figure 2-2: The use of artificial fertiliser is set to hold pace with an increasing world population[16]

Poverty is No One's Choice but What Kind of Lifestyle Do We Want?

Everybody wants some comfort in their life. Although largely outdated, this was first addressed by Maslow's hierarchy of basic needs.[17] The physiological needs (access to food, water and air) as well as the need for clothing and shelter are the most basic needs for human beings. Unfortunately, throughout history a fair proportion of us has not enjoyed a fulfilment of these basic needs: Even now, globally almost 870 million people are chronically

---

[16] http://large.stanford.edu/courses/2014/ph240/yuan2/. Fertiliser data from FAO

[17] *A Theory of Human Motivation* by A.H. Maslow, Martino Fine books, 2013 reprint.

undernourished.[18] However percentage-wise there is a dramatic improvement in recent years (see Figure 2-3):

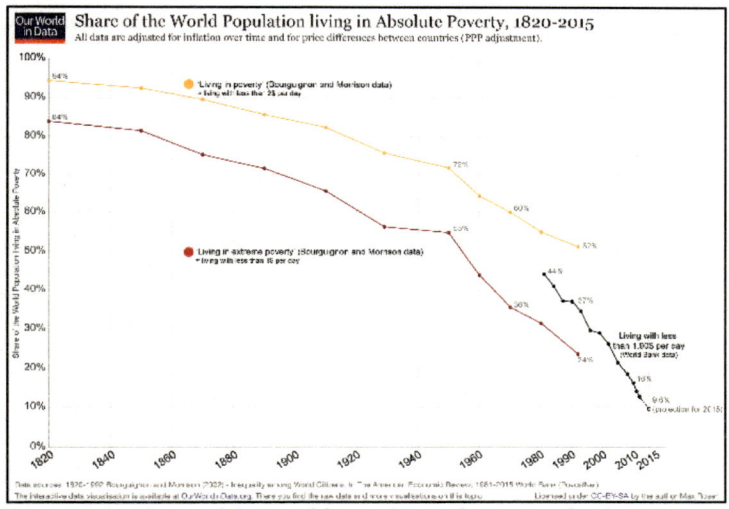

Figure 2-3: Share of the world population living in absolute poverty over the last 200 years[19]

It is not clear from the prehistoric record how many of the people were living in poverty in hunter-gatherer days. The concept of poverty is up for debate, and opinions differ when linking poverty to a daily monetary amount to spend. Opinions differ even more to define poverty in pre-historic times, when monetary units were absent.

The absolute poverty records as from the 19th century show a remarkable trend: due to the advent of cheap energy and a string of medical discoveries, improving sanitation, the percentage of people living below the poverty line started to drop gradually but significantly (see Figure 2-3), even whilst the world population was rising significantly. In other words, the world population rose

[18] (http://www.fao.org/news/story/en/item/161819/icode/
[19] Max Roser and Esteban Ortiz-Ospina (2017) – *'Global Extreme Poverty'*. Published online at OurWorldInData.org. Retrieved from: https://ourworldindata.org/extreme-poverty/

and the people in absolute poverty rose, but the latter did not rise as fast as the world population. However, the major percentage drop of people living in absolute poverty started after the Green Revolution in the 1960s with the industrial application of artificial fertiliser, impacting crop yield on a massive scale.

No one wants to live in poverty that is clear enough, but is everything bliss once above the absolute poverty line? Maslow's mentioned other needs, which need fulfilment to lead a happy life. Maslow's original work has been updated and replaced by a more modern framework of concepts. The concept of 'Quality of Life' with corresponding indicators is more common now to define well-being.

But again 'Quality of Life' is hard to define: cultural differences prevail and the concept is often used commercially by rating agencies to compare cities or countries, almost exclusively with a western bias. And, very little is known to compare 'Quality of Life' throughout time. How does our current 'Quality of Life' compare with the people living in the Stone Age, Middle Ages or in the 19th century? In a dictionary for business terms, I have found a standard, rather general and unbiased definition for 'Quality of Life':

"Daily living enhanced by wholesome food and clean air and water, enjoyment of unfettered open spaces and bodies of water, conservation of wildlife and natural resources, security from crime, and protection from radiation and toxic substances. It may also be used as a measure of the energy and power a person is endowed with that enable him or her to enjoy life and prevail over life's challenges irrespective of the handicaps he or she may have." [20]

In an attempt to quantify changes over time, I have simplified the above definition into several categories:

- Availability of healthy food, clean air and water
- Security from wars and crime

[20] http://www.businessdictionary.com/definition/quality-of-life.html

- Enjoyment of the environment
- Protection from pollution
- Availability/Affordability of sufficient energy

In Figure 2-4, I have attempted to indicate trends of the five above mentioned 'Quality of Life' indicators in relation to the three major events of population growth (Agricultural, Industrial and Green Revolutions).

The availability of healthy food, clean water and air is gradually improving over time (red curve in Figure 2-4), although lumping the three ingredients (reminiscent of Maslow's physiological needs) is disguising individual trends (e.g. availability of clean water is certainly deteriorating over time). It is my perception that we have already reached a maximum and that in particular quality and availability of clean air and water are decreasing over the last decades for the world as a whole (e.g. smog in Beijing, persistent droughts in Africa).

The security from wars and crime (blue curve in Figure 2-4) is gradually improving in percentage terms over the ages. We have become less violent, refer to footnote 12. There is some debate whether violence is really reducing and what effect this has on us.[21] Moreover, did crime really reduce over the ages? And how to define crime? Violent crime may be waning, but due to globalisation white-collar crime (legal or not…) has proliferated immensely and has created a whole new sense of insecurity. A large part of us are now victims of economic downturns, caused by an elite banking sector. The loss of property in the bursting of the housing bubble in the USA and the loss of money in Iceland or Cyprus are recent examples of this. Also, suicide bombing and terrorism are new phenomena with sophisticated means to maximise casualties.

The enjoyment of the environment (green curve in Figure 2-4) is gradually decreasing from our halcyon hunter-gatherer days. Massive reduction in primordial forests to clear land for agriculture and later for mining, resulted in an equally massive

---

[21] http://www.theguardian.com/commentisfree/2011 /nov/08/steven-pinker-better-angels-of-our-nature

drop in biodiversity. And our sheer numbers, living in cities, are also pushing nature away. There are city dwellers which have never seen a domesticated animal used for food production, let alone a wild one. Agriculture has become more and more intense, straining the wild population of animals and plants even more. Consequently, rare animals and plants can only be admired in dedicated parks and zoos.

Protection from pollution (brown curve in Figure 2-4) has seen a dramatic drop as of the start of the Industrial Revolution. Images of smog over coal-fired houses in London and lifeless rivers with untreated sewage are well-known. Due to very large-scale industries to supply the world population with products and abject poverty, these polluting situations still exist in the developing world (e.g. recurrent smog in Beijing and heavy polluted bays in Rio de Janeiro, used for rowing matches during the 2016 Olympic Games). In the developed world, some improvement has been made combatting air pollution due to strict regulation. However, the massive use of diesel cars frequently causes city pollution to break regulatory limits.[22]

The orange curve in Figure 2-4 refers to the availability and affordability of energy. In general, with the advent of the industrial revolution, global energy needs are met. But not for all of us. Very recently, deaths from extreme temperatures because of climatic changes are on the rise. Although access to energy has increased dramatically over the last 200 years, more than 1.2 billion people across the world still lack access to electricity while a further 2.8 billion have no choice, other than traditional biomass for cooking and heating.[23]

---

[22] https://www.theguardian.com/environment /2016/feb/05/the-truth-about-londons-air-pollution

[23] http://www.sciencedirect.com/science/article/pii /S221462961500078X

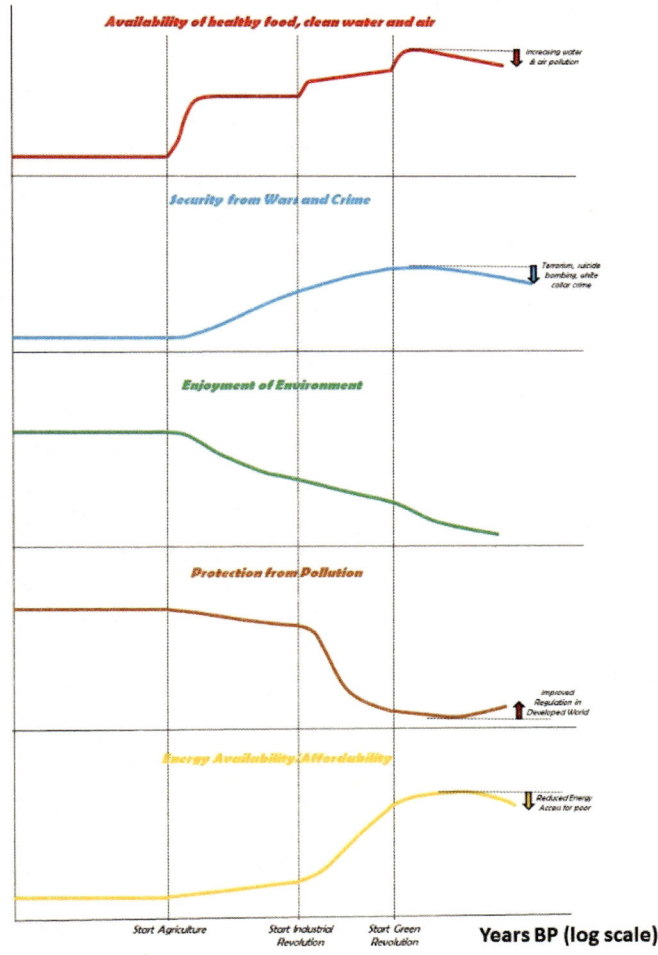

Figure 2-4: Qualitative trends of five 'Quality of Life' indicators over time (non-linear time scale)

Access to energy is no problem in the developed world, but affordability of energy is not always automatic. Fuel poverty (when more than 10% of one's income is needed to be spent on heating and cooking) is a relative new phenomenon in the developed world. It is realised that fuel poverty is predominantly the result of a recent rising inequality.

In summary, inspecting the quality of life of mankind over the last 200 years, it is noted that on one hand modern times provide a better quality of life, but on the other hand this comes at extra costs. A ballooning world population starts to interfere significantly with our quality of life, increasing pollution and environmental pressures, loss of biodiversity and rise in crime. Our global living standards are under pressure.

Higher Living Standards for Everybody— Can the Planet Afford Those?

Living standards are difficult to measure. Gross domestic product (GDP) is considered too crude a measure. GDP is not capturing all economic activity, such as child minding by mothers, whilst GDP captures disproportionally the living standards of the money generating rich part of the population. *'Whose GDP?'* is a valid question for the millions who have not seen any sensible pay rise since the financial crisis of 2008. A more refined number is the Human Development Index (HDI), which is a composite statistic of life expectancy, education, and income per capita.[24] However, correlations between HDI and energy use per capita are not well established yet, whilst the relationship between GDP and Energy use is well known (see Figure 2-5).

Although the GDP of the United States is 50% higher than the countries in the European Union (2011 data, see Figure 2-5), the current HDI is similar, despite the energy use being more than double. To raise the world's HDI or GDP to say European levels, would require significant increase in energy use per capita (more than 50% according to Figure 2-5). At the current stage, this does not seem doable, due to limited resources on the planet. And an increasing population, predominantly in developing countries with low energy use per capita, is weighing on this even more. Are we stuck in an unequal world due to limitations of available

---

[24]https://en.wikipedia.org/wiki/List_of_countries_by_Human_Development_Index

energy? The only way out seems to apply energy conservation on a massive scale to achieve an average lower energy use globally whilst simultaneously and rapidly introduce renewable energy.

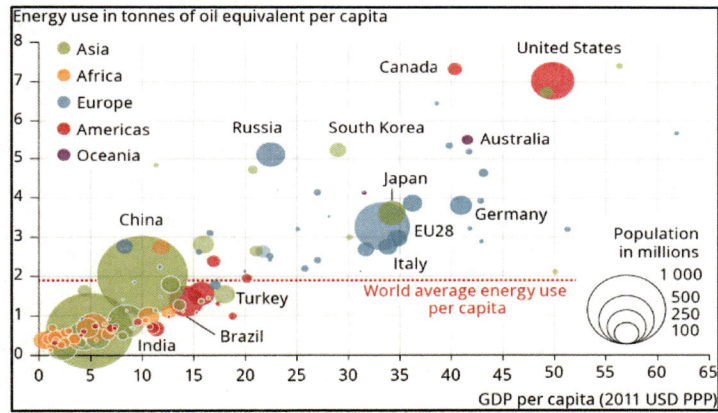

Figure 2-5: Increasing GDP is requiring an increased energy use[25]

This limited affordability which the planet provides us seems like the limited affordability of a more equal world.[26] As with limits to the planetary riches and limits to global temperatures, the economic riches are finite as well. Moreover, a strong link exists between the riches of the planet and the riches of mankind. Trying to squeeze inequality beyond boundaries is a recipe for revolutions just like it is dangerous pushing the planetary limits beyond tipping points, causing irreversible temperature changes, loss of biodiversity and habitat. So, let us have a closer look on inequality and its relationship with fertility rate.

Income Equality

The world is very unequal. A period of reduced income inequality in the world existed in the period 1945–1980, but since the start of the neoliberalism of Thatcher and Reagan, inequality

---

[25]http://www.eea.europa.eu/data-and-maps/figures/correlation-of-per-capita-energy

[26] *Inequality and the 1%*. Danny Dorling (2014)

started to rise again.[27] When correlating the widely-used equality index, GINI, versus the fertility rate, it is noteworthy that a positive relationship occurs: The more unequal a country is (high GINI), the higher the fertility rate (see Figure 2-6).

What is noteworthy in Figure 2-6 is that several, mainly African, countries are not on this trend (highlighted and named in red). Since they also represent the poorest countries in the world, the fertility rate is more dominated by their respective low HDI or GDP, although I must admit that I found the relatively low GINI indices surprising for these countries. Most of these countries also have a high Corruption Perception Index (or CPI[28]) and the rich in those countries have probably large amounts of money stashed away in tax havens, which does not show in the official numbers. The GINI indices for these countries seem almost certainly higher.

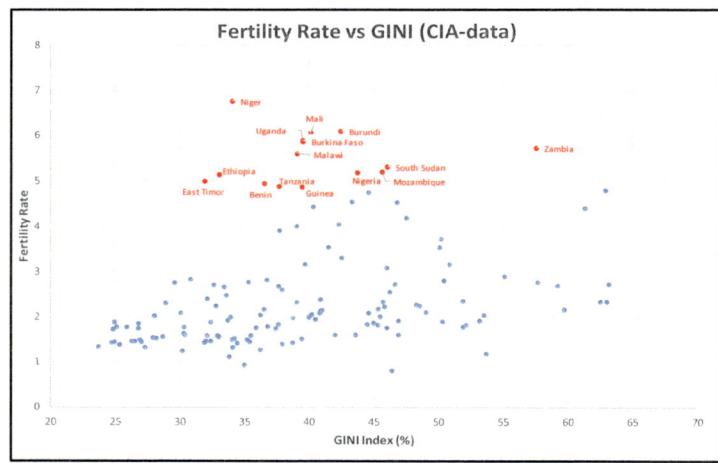

Figure 2-6: Correlation between GINI index and Fertility Rate[29]

[27] *Capital in the Twenty First Century*. Thomas Piketty (2014)

[28] http://www.transparency.org/cpi2015

[29] GINI from various dates from CIA data, published in https://en.wikipedia.org/wiki/List_of_countries_by_income_equality and 2015 fertility rate data from https://en.wikipedia.org/wiki/List_of_sovereign_states_and_dependent_terri tories_by_fertility_rate (CIA Fact book data)

From Figure 2-6 a clear trend is visible that higher inequality correlates positively with fertility rate and thus a growing population. This suggests that inequality feeds a growing world population. How about the inverse trend? Could a growing world population cause increased inequality? With planetary and consequently economic wealth limited, this could be a possibility. Most of the world population is added in the poorer part of the income distribution and the rich are very protective not to share (with justification we say that the rich get richer). Figure 2-7 is suggesting such a global trend over the last 200 years, whilst the trend is still visible over a shorter timeframe for US, UK and China.

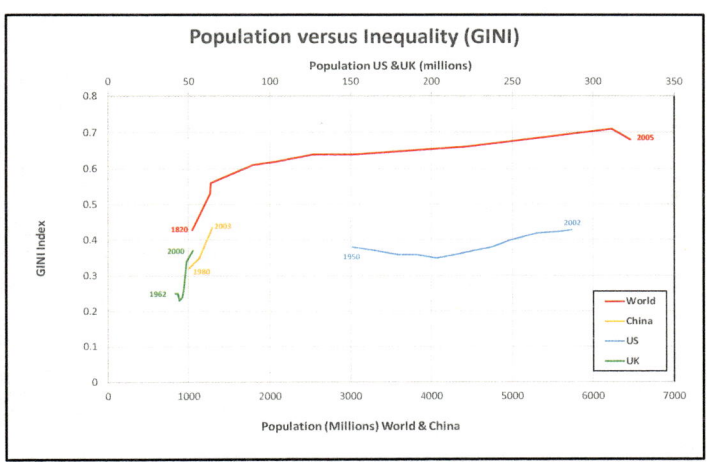

Figure 2-7: Does an increasing world population create more inequality? Data suggest that there is a strong trend [30]

To back up my claim of increasing inequality with increasing population, an artificial exercise was carried out by introducing an extra three billion people into the lower two deciles of the income distribution of the world, something which is likely to happen during the 21st century. This was done via a Lorenz plot, which relates in a normalised way the share of global resources versus

---

[30] https://en.wikipedia.org/wiki/Gini_coefficient

the share of the global population. The GINI index is related to the area between the 45-degree line and the curve (Figure 2-8). Adding another three billion in the two lower deciles, makes this area larger, an indication of increasing GINI index and hence increasing inequality.

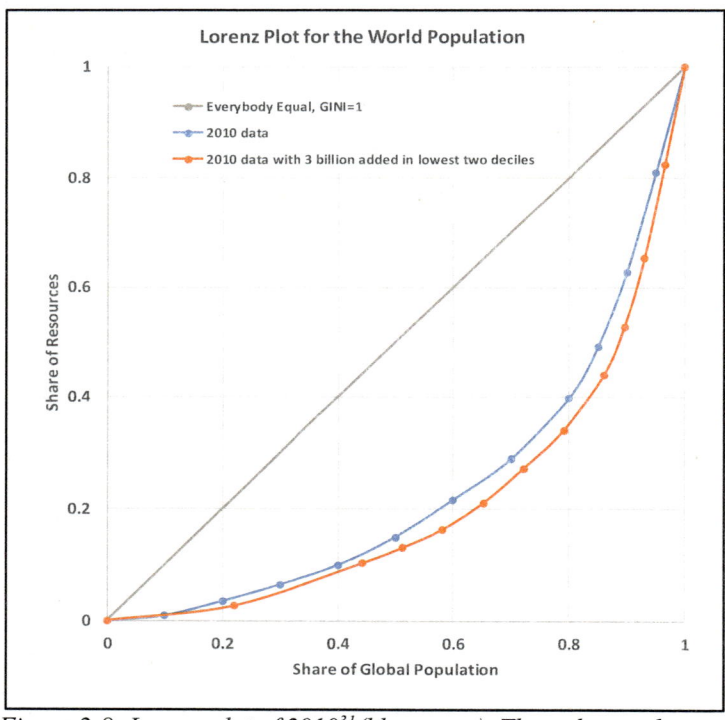

Figure 2-8: Lorenz plot of 2010[31](blue curve). The red curve has been modified introducing an additional 3 billion people at the lowest two deciles by means of de-normalisation and renormalisation. The effect is an increasing inequality (or GINI index = area between the 45-degree line and the Lorenz curve).

[31]http://www.du.edu/ifs/help/use-online/display/specialized/worldmap.html

Gender Equality

Fertility rate is not only increasing income inequality. Not surprisingly a higher fertility rate also causes higher gender inequality (and vice versa). To estimate the effect on gender equality, the fertility rate was correlated against the gender inequality index (GII)[32] (see Figure 2-9). The GII is a relatively new index made up by effects on women's health, empowerment and participation in the labour market.

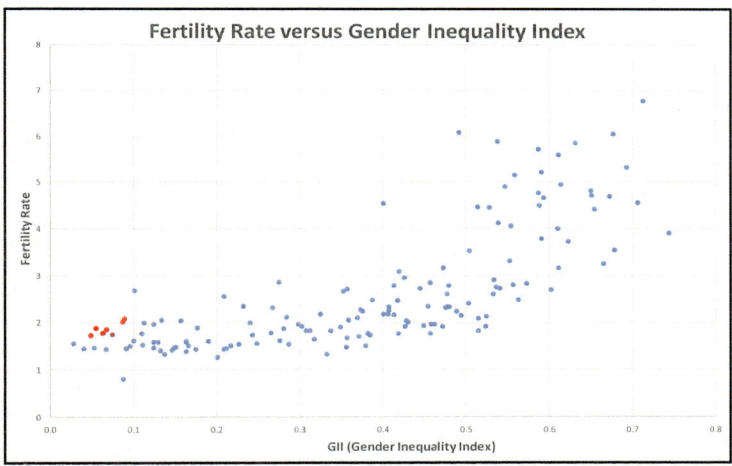

Figure 2-9: Fertility rate versus Gender Inequality index (data from refs 14 and 18). The red points are from countries where childcare is well organised and cheap (Scandinavia, Benelux and France).

It is noted that the fertility rate only starts to increase considerably above a GII of 0.4 to 0.5 and that fertility rate is relatively independent on gender equality below that number. In fact, there is evidence that fertility is rising slightly for extreme gender-equal countries, with a positive attitude to working

[32] https://en.wikipedia.org/wiki/Gender_Inequality_ Index#cite_note-2012GII-11

women[33] and provision of cheap good quality childcare.[34] It is striking that in this best possible scenario for women (very low inequality) fertility is hovering close to the replacement ratio of two.

Sarah Harper mentions a heart-breaking story from Niger of a young girl, Samira.[35] With only primary school education, like 98% of the girls in Niger, she was married at 13 years to a 52-year-old man. She gave birth to nine children. All her four daughters married at 13 years as well and at 27 years, Samira became a grandmother and a widow at 28 years. She and her family are now completely dependent on her husband's family.

Do we need to grow?

Growth is imbedded in our recent thinking. As a species, we always seem to want more. This adage is very visible in our neo-liberal capitalist society of the last 35 years. We are focussed on GDP growth, independent of our planetary limits. Green thinking on zero growth or using steady state economics[36] is not being taken very seriously. Note that one of the concepts of steady state economics is a constant population. With an ever-increasing population, we cannot reach a steady state between ourselves and the environment of our planet, something which in the end will become unsustainable.

Population growth has been promoted throughout the ages by the Church and contraception methods have been discouraged. Although religious arguments are employed to defend this, there is also a more cynical view that for centuries the church has teamed up with rich land owners and later factory owners, who needed a large proletariat to maintain their elitist lifestyle. In the past, the religious class used a large workforce as well to build

---

[33] http://www.oecdobserver.org/news/archivestory. php/aid/1664/Does_gender_equality_spur_growth_.html

[34] "Indeed, the map of fertility rates in the EU is remarkably similar to that of childcare facilities", http://www.theguardian.com/world/2015/mar/21/france-population-europe-fertility-rate

[35] *How Population Change Will Transform Our World*. Sarah Harper (2016). Oxford University Press, p. 7.

[36] *Steady State Economics*. Herman Daly (2nd edition, 1992)

rich monasteries or immense cathedrals, whilst bishops and cardinals lived like princes and kings.

Anthropocentrism

So far, we have only talked about the impact of over-population on other human beings. A number of recent books[37,38] on population, strictly talk about the effects between humans, without considering planetary limits or other species on the planet. Demographers seem wary of going into the domain of environmentalism or sustainable economics whilst environmentalists seem wary of facing inconvenient questions about population. As a species, we are much advantaged that we can talk and write about the effects on us. Unfortunately, a white rhinoceros, tiger or blue-fin tuna have no say in what is done to their habitats. Due to our growing numbers, there is immense pressure on other species.

What moral justification do we have to put ourselves first? We have become gods and have shaped this planet beyond recognition. Many authors already speak of the Anthropocene, where everything is conquered and the surface of the earth is altered in support of human convenience (roads, dams, endless fields with monoculture).

Yet we do need other species to fulfil our enjoyment and marvel of the environment. Therefore, we maintain national parks and dedicated wilderness areas. A lack of biodiversity is dangerous because more and more food species are genetically modified and the more specialised they become, the more vulnerable they will be to a specialised disease. The loss in numbers per capita and species is extremely worrying (see Table 2-1). A decrease in biodiversity manifests itself in habitat loss, over-exploitation or invasions of alien species and indirectly by pollution and climate change. It is time to have a look at that in a bit more detail.

---

[37] *How Population Change Will Transform Our World*. Sarah Harper (2016). Oxford University Press
[38] *Peoplequake*. Fred Pearce (2011). Eden Project Books

POPULATION AND AVAILABILITY OF RENEWABLE RESOURCES				
	1990	**2010**	**Total Change (%)**	**Per Capita Change (%)**
Population (M)	5290	7030	33	
Fish Catch (Mtonnes)	85	102	20	-10
Irrigated Land (Mha)	237	277	17	-12
Cropland (Mha)	1444	1516	5	-21
Rangeland and Pasture (Mha)	3402	3540	4	-22
Forests (Mha)	3413	3165	-7	-30

Table 2-1: A snapshot over 20 years, where population increases by 33%. An increase in land use, fish catch and a decrease in forest cover is noticed. Per capita they all decrease.[39]

[39] *Taking Nature into Account.* A report to the Club of Rome. Wouter van Dieren (2012) p.51

Chapter 3
Environmental Pressures

When I was a boy I played with my brothers and friends in the woods behind our housing estate on the outskirts of the town I grew up in. In the woods, we made huts, watched animals, played hide and seek and made war with another gang of boys, like a tribe of chimpanzees. The housing estate was new and before the houses were built, there were woods and meadows. Ten years later the woods with everything in it was gone and replaced by yet another housing estate for an expanding population. I feel melancholic, thinking about that and I am not the only one. With the disappearance of the woods, the birds, rabbits, hedgehogs and foxes disappeared as well.

This is not a story on its own; I have heard countless others and read about a million more. It is not just sadness about the loss of animals or beautiful nature; it is also that we as human beings are deprived of habitats for our enjoyment or play. It is sad to see young urban children with hardly a place to play or who have never seen even the most common wild animals. This trend is aggravating with the advent of high-rise buildings, television, computer games and mobile telephones.

Our love for nature has been expressed in numerous books from the early Greeks to Thoreau's Walden. And nature programmes are amongst the most popular on television.

Extinctions

We are not alone on Planet Earth. However, there is a strong correlation between the growth in human population and extinction of other species (see Figure 3-1). Note the tipping point in the number of extinctions after 1960, when the world population started to increase dramatically because of the Green Revolution. It was the Green Revolution which started the domination of monoculture and which killed loads of species by the intensive use of pesticides and herbicides.

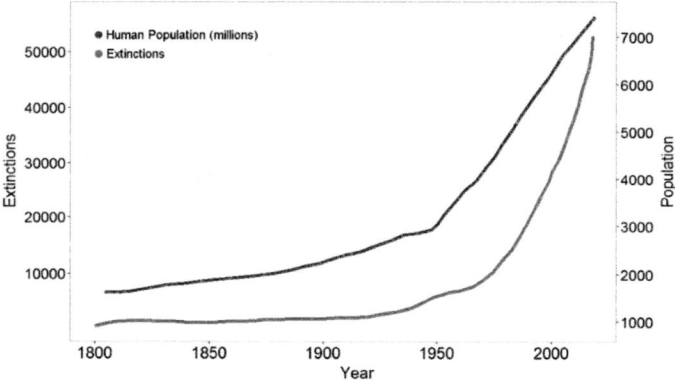

Figure 3-1: The number of species, going extinct over the last 200 years goes hand in hand with a growth in human population[40]

Although we are animals with an instinct to dominate and who have carved out a survival niche on this planet, we are also the only advanced conscious species with a sense of morality. The transition between the Enlightenment and the Industrial Revolution is earmarked by the start of Capitalism. Adam Smith happened to write his treaty '*The Wealth of Nations*' in 1776 when James Watt produced his first commercial steam engine.[41] The idea of liberation from and domination of nature has its roots in the Enlightenment and further back in Christian values.[42]

---

[40] Scott, J. Michael, Slides: "*Threats to Biological Diversity: Global, Continental, Local*" (2008). Shifting Base lines and New Meridians: Water, Resources, Landscapes, and the Transformation of the American West Summer Conference, June 4-6)

[41] Naomi Klein. *This Changes Everything* (2014) Penguin edition p. 173.

[42] "*Then God said, "Let us make man in our image, after our likeness. And let them have dominion over the fish of the sea and over the birds of the*

However, another Christian meaning for 'mastering nature' is to act as a custodian or steward of nature.[43] Instead, this more philosophical and positive attitude has been pushed in the background, whilst Capitalism fired our passion for greed.

Some authors mention this recent unprecedented extinction the 'Sixth Mass Extinction'. Five mass extinctions preceded during the 600 million years of life on earth (see Figure 3-2). They were all caused by external factors such as comet impacts, global warming events and consequent massive climate changes. All five preceding historical mass extinctions took a considerable amount of time (thousands of years), whilst our man-made mass extinction is taken not more than a couple of hundred years. The sixth mass extinction is therefore without precedent.

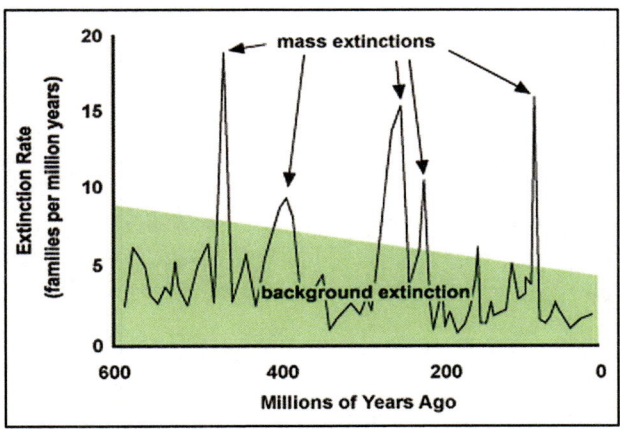

Figure 3-2: Five mass extinctions during the 600 million years of life have preceded the current one.[44]

heavens and over the livestock and over all the earth and over every creeping thing that creeps on the earth."" Genesis 1:26

[43] "As each has received a gift, use it to serve one another, as good stewards of God's varied grace" 1 Peter 4:10.

[44] University of California Museum of Palaeontology. http://evolution.berkeley.edu/evolibrary/search/imagedetail.php?id=351&topic_id=&keywords=

Habitat Loss, Alteration or Degradation

To date, about 50 percent of the planet's natural habitats have been cleared for human use and another 0.5 to 1.5 percent of nature is lost each year.[45] Animals lose their territory because humans encroach by constructing roads[46], towns and dams, and large species fragment by large scale fencing (see Figure 3-3). Habitat alteration or degradation is caused for example by laying dams in rivers for electricity generation or to improve a constant water supply. A large part of river habitats has been lost with increasing human populations and in some countries, there are hardly any river habitats left (e.g. Spain, China, Egypt). At best river habitats make place for lake habitats.

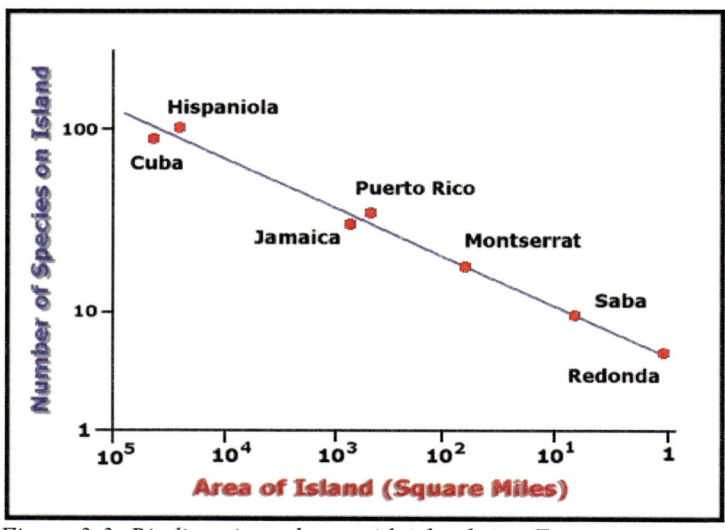

Figure 3-3: Biodiversity reduces with island size. Fragmentation due to roads, railways and large-scale fencing can have the same effect for larger species.[47]

[45]https://www.learner.org/courses/envsci/unit/text.php?unit=9&secNum=6
[46]https://www.theguardian.com/environment/2016/dec/15/new-map-reveals-shattering-effect-of-roads-on-nature
[47]http://www.globalchange.umich.edu/globalchange2/current/lectures/biodiversity/biodiversity.html

Habitat loss is not everywhere the same. Figure 3-4 suggests that extreme habitats, where human occupation is limited, such as tundra and boreal forest remain largely intact. On the other hand, Mediterranean and temperate forest habitats have already lost 70% of their area since the time, when human beings started to convert woodlands to agriculture and to supply fuel and wood for construction. Note that a reduction in tropical habitats is relatively recent, with growing needs (or greeds?) for wood, open pit mining and oil and gas exploration and production. The loss in desert habitat in Figure 3-4 seems strange: although there are some agricultural efforts in the Gulf States, relying heavily on irrigation, a lot of desert is added by overgrazing or erosion due to excessive tilling of low precipitation regions.

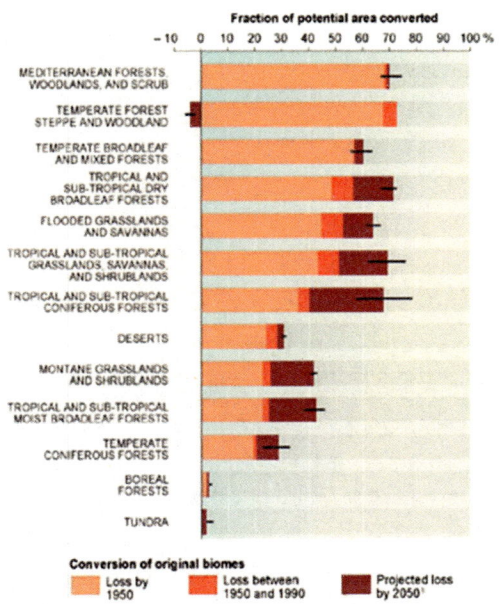

Figure 3-4: Losses of various habitats over time.[48] Loss in Desert habitat seems strange, since a lot of desert is added

[48] 2005. World Resources Institute. Millennium Ecosystem Assessment. *Ecosystems and Human Well-Being: Synthesis*, p.4 (Washington, DC: Island Press).

Habitat loss or alteration can also occur by keeping increasing number of livestock. It is well known that goats and sheep encourage desertification in drier climates and promote soil erosion in wetter climates.[49] Figure 3-5 shows that not only the human population more than doubled over the period 1961–2013, but significant amounts of livestock were added not only to feed the extra population but also to provide a largely hungry existing population with an improved diet. After all we are increasingly able to assure our food production, but we also have more people to feed (see Green Revolution, chapter 2).

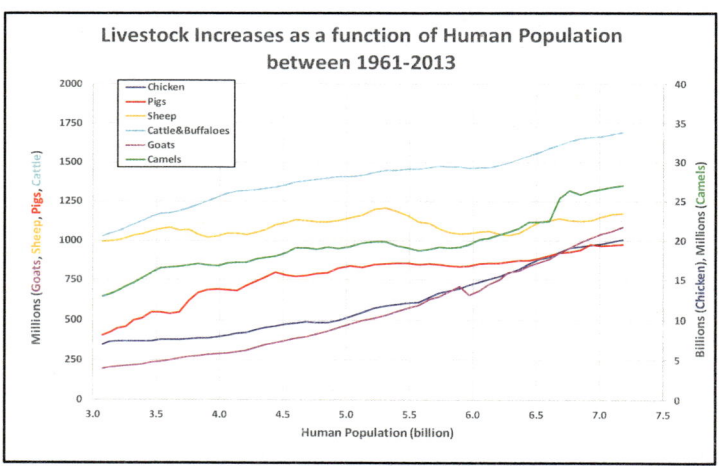

Figure 3-5: Increases in livestock as a function of human population growth over the last 50 years[50]

Over Exploitation/Hunting

Although we are no longer hunter-gatherers, we still have an appetite for wild food. For centuries, we have supplemented our agricultural diet with hunting or gathering berries in the woods. Gradually hunting became an aristocratic past-time, later joined by nouveau-riche industrialists and bankers.

---

[49] *Feral: Searching for Enchantment on the Frontiers of Rewilding.* George Monbiot (2013)

[50] http://faostat.fao.org/site/573/DesktopDefault.aspx? PageID=573#ancor

The past is full of evidence that we are expert hunters. We managed to extinguish the large and easy prey when entering pristine areas during pre-historic times such as Northern Europe or North America after the ice age. All large mega-fauna disappeared within a relatively short time-span. And we repeated that again in North America with a second wave of occupation, where we managed to almost extinguish the bison (discussed later). Our historical response to the absence of hunting prey for food has been to get rid of competitor hunting species such as the wolf, fox, eagle or lion. Again, we were very successful bringing these species to near-extinction.

Gradually we started to semi-domesticate wild species by setting up large areas as hunting grounds, specifically to hunt one species only. Examples of this are red deer or grouse with disastrous consequences for other species or causing failures in water management.[51] But supply of food from wild animals became less important in recent days and these estates were kept as pleasure grounds for trigger-happy hunters only. It is a pity sight to see millions of pheasants raised and fed like chicken to be subsequently shot at by myopic bankers or run over by uncaring motorists.

Fishing is another form of hunting. We manage to fish the seas almost empty and needed to intensely regulate fishing in Europe to prevent extinction of an important staple food. But even now the seas and lakes are so overfished that we need to resort to fish farming for our demand in fish. This relatively recent addition to agriculture (or aquaculture) is one more step into the direction of a dangerous food dependency (see Figure 3-6). With the ballooning world population, we are no longer able to supply our demands by wild salmon alone. The vulnerability of aquaculture is only highlighted by new threats such as the sea lice infestation of salmon farms, causing a chemical arms race.[52] This is just an example, similar trends are noticeable with GM-crops, with intense pig, cattle or poultry farming, which are all necessary to

---

[51]http://www.theguardian.com/commentisfree/2015 /dec/29/deluge-farmers-flood-grouse-moor-drain-land

[52]https://www.theguardian.com/environment/2017/ apr/01/is-farming-salmon-bad-for-the-environment

give us a balanced diet. We can no longer do without this artificiality and intensification; there is no way back to the past.

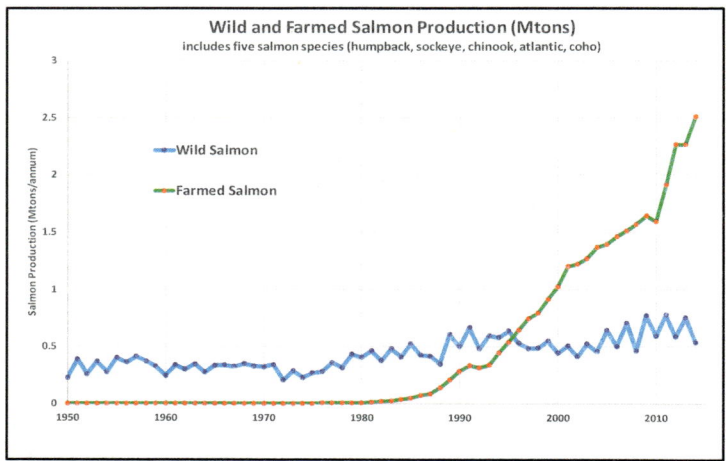

Figure 3-6: Salmon farming kicked off some 40 years ago. Graph is in millions of tonnes. We are now farming twice as many salmon as catching wild salmon.[53]

An additional risks of intense farming methods with altered varieties (albeit with or without genetic modification) is the contamination of the wild species by sheer numbers near intense farming locations. This is a key threat to biodiversity and a potential worry for future, yet unidentified diseases.

But it is not only food we hunted for: when conquering the plains of North America, the first European colonists noticed a vast potential in the bison they encountered. Native Americans lived in harmony with approximately 60 million bison. Within the course of a century numbers dropped to less than a thousand (see Figure 3-7). Bison were predominantly hunted for their fur and

---

[53] Based on data sourced from the relevant FAO Species Fact Sheets for period 1950-2014 for five salmon species (Sockeye, Humpback, Chinook, Coho and Atlantic salmon)

leather, whilst their ground bones found a destination as fertiliser[54].

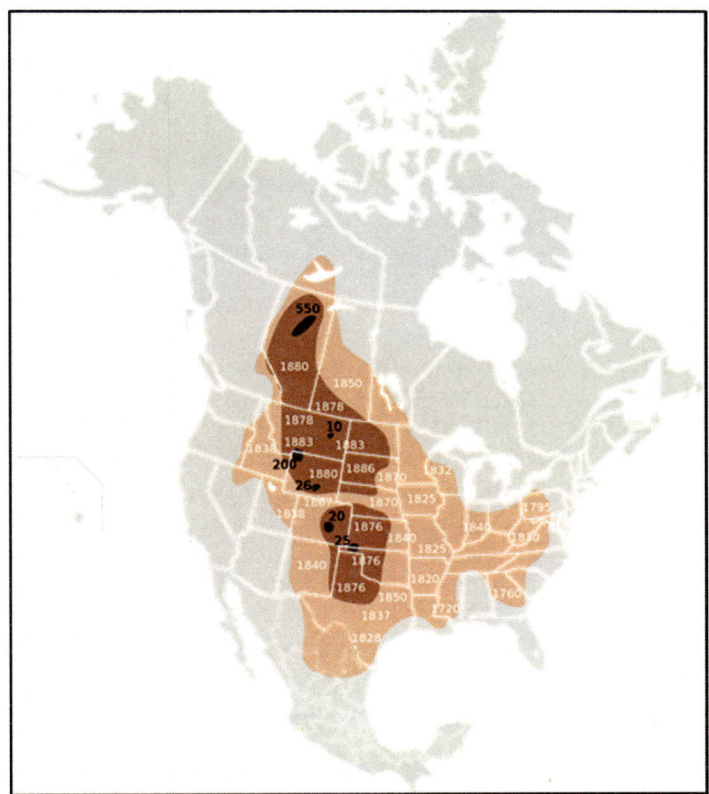

Figure 3-7: Extermination of the American Bison. Original range (buff), range in 1870 (brown) and the smallest population left in 1889 (dark brown). Dark brown numbers are 1889 numbers left. Since then numbers have risen to 360,000.[55]

[54] *Records, Laban (March 1995). Cherokee Outlet Cowboy: Recollections of Laban S. Records.* Norman, Oklahoma: University of Oklahoma Press. ISBN 978-0-8061-2694-4.
[55] https://en.wikipedia.org/wiki/American_bison, adapted by user Cephas from a drawing of William Temple Hornaday in "*Geographisches*

A similar fate met the whales which were hunted almost exclusively for their oil and only recently whales are killed exclusively for food. Over the course of 200 years, worldwide whale numbers amounted to 1.5 million and have declined dramatically to around 20,000 now.[56] Even more tragic is the decline in animal species, hunted for curiosa: rhinoceros horn (believed to be an aphrodisiac), elephant tusks (carving) and shark fins (luxury cuisine item) are some examples. Predominantly China and its neighbours are the main markets for these goods. Obviously, this had dramatic effects on the population of these animals and some of them are near extinction.

Pollution

The increasing world population has caused a large variety of pollution. The solid wastes of massive piles of rubbish or slagheaps from the mining industry were a familiar sight some 50 years ago. Due to improved regulation in the developed nations, we managed to increase our recycling efforts dramatically by processing our waste differently, such as incineration or reducing solid waste. Unfortunately, a lively waste trade exists from developed countries to the developing ones and this waste is often the more harmful one (e.g. toxic chemicals).

It is expected that the solid waste we generate will triple by the end of this century.[57] The main rise in solid waste is expected where population will rise fastest (Sub-Saharan Africa and South Asia) and for the lower middle incomes (see Figure 3-8). There is a boom in recycling and incineration (waste to energy). However, incineration is not such a clean method; some of the incineration ash is hazardous waste, due to high metal and organic contents and the burning of waste adds CO_2 to the atmosphere. A lot of spare incineration capacity was built in Europe, causing a reduced need

Handbuch zu Andrees Handatlas, vierte Auflage, Bielefeld und Leipzig, Velhagen und Klasing, 1902"

[56]http://news.stanford.edu/news/2003/august6/whales-86.html

[57] Waste Production Must Peak this Century. D. Hoornweg, P. Bhada-Tata, C. Kennedy. Nature, 30 October 2013.

for recycling (with less incineration capacity recycling could have been higher).[58]

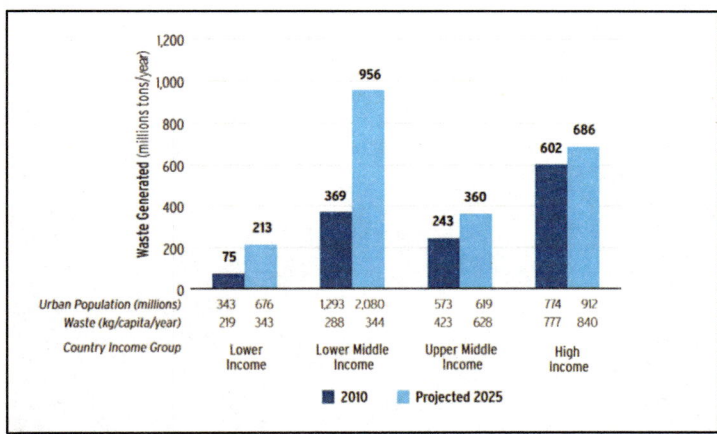

Figure 3-8: Expected Waste Production for three different scenarios[59]

Plastic waste in particular will be a problem in the future, since we are using it increasingly for packaging. While most plastics are touted as recyclable, the reality is that they are 'down-cycled': a plastic milk carton can never be recycled into another carton; it can be made into a lower-quality item like plastic lumber, which cannot be recycled.[60] There are different types of plastics, which cannot be recycled altogether and separation is difficult. As a result, 50% of plastics are still landfilled in the EU[61] and in the developing world the number is likely to be very much higher. We also have thrown so much plastic away in the environment that rivers and oceans are permanently polluted with

[58] http://e360.yale.edu/feature/incineration_versus_recycling__in_europe_a_debate_over_trash/2686/

[59] *What a Waste: A global review of solid waste management* by D. Hoornweg and P. Bhada Tata. Worldbank Urban Development series, March 2012, No. 15. Figure 3.

[60] http://www.mnn.com/lifestyle/responsible-living/stories/16-simple-ways-reduce-plastic-waste

[61] ttp://ec.europa.eu/environment/waste/plastic_waste.htm

plastic waste, since plastic only degrades very slowly. The plastic particles are forming a plastic soup (see Figure 3-9) and are polluting large areas of water, affecting wildlife. Recycling of plastics should be strongly promoted, by increasing legislation and taxation (less use of plastics in packaging and to use less types of plastics, so recycling is made easier).

Figure 3-9: Our plastic waste over the last 50 years is accumulating in the oceans

Liquid waste is also increasing dramatically; it originates from human waste, agricultural waste (excess pesticides and fertilisers) or chemical wastes in all degrees and concentrations. Eighty percent of all wastewater in the world goes untreated.[62] Admittedly, some wastewater is valuable, due to presence of nutrients and is reused wherever possible. However, a lot of the nutritious wastewater finds its way to rivers and coasts (e.g. leaching of fertiliser) due to excess rainfall or because of too costly transportation (i.e. manure sludge from industrial farming). In those cases, the water gets atrophied causing algal blooms (see Figure 3-10) and death of fish and other aquatic animals.

---

[62]http://www.unwater.org/fileadmin/user_upload/unwater_new/docs/UN-Water_Analytical_Brief_Wastewater_Management.pdf

Nitrogen fertiliser is overused by 30 to 60 percent in intensive managed fields in China.[63] Mark Lynas mentioned limits for man-made nitrogen and phosphor in his book *The God Species*,[64] but the limits are arbitrary and in case of nitrogen already surpassed by a factor of 3.5. The environmental damage of industrial scale nitrogen use is multi-facetted and not very well understood, since we have only been using it for 50–60 years. Its use causes a loss of biodiversity; the production process of fertiliser produces extra CO_2; Industrial scale Nitrogen use causes air pollution by NO_x and an increase in greenhouse gases (N_2O is very potent).

Figure 3-10: Algal Bloom

Water pollution is not limited to pumping polluting agents into the water. When CO_2 is increasing in the atmosphere, it will dissolve partly in the water of the oceans, causing acidification. This in turn causes decalcification of shellfish and bleaching of corals, followed by death. Prior to the Industrial Revolution, the pH of the oceans has been slightly alkaline, averaging about 8.2. Today it is around 8.1, a drop of 0.1 pH units, representing a 29% increase in acidity over the past two centuries (see Table 3-1).

Perhaps the most easily identified form of pollution is air pollution, since it has affected us so directly. In the past London was reliant on coal for heating and the dense smog has caused

[63] http://ngm.nationalgeographic.com/2013/05/fertilized-world/charles-text
[64] *The God Species* by Mark Lynas (2011) Fourth Estate books. p.235

many deaths. Since coal burning was banned, air quality has improved. However, large scale coal burning for electricity generation in modern day China, has seen a repeat of air pollution in Beijing.

Air pollution from transport is not diminishing. Admittedly air pollution is also caused by increased economic activity and not just as an effect of an increasing population, but it is difficult to split the effect to either of the two influences. In particular, older diesel engines emit air-born fines (particulates) and increased shipping[65] emits a lot more polluting agents due to laxer regulation when at sea. A large cruise ship emits as many air pollutants as five million cars over the same distance.[66] Because of increased economic activity and an increased world population, shipping is forecasted to increase significantly.[67]

Time	pH	(pH)	H^+ Concentration increase	Source
18th Century	8.179			
1990's	8.104	-0.075	+18.9%	
Present	8.069	-0.110	+28.8%	
2050	7.949	-0.230	+69.8%	Based on 560 ppm CO_2 in atmosphere
2100	7.824	-0.355	+126.5%	Based on 788 ppm CO_2 in atmosphere (IS92a scenario[68])

Table 3-1: Recorded and expected changes in Ocean Acidity[69]

[65] The world merchant fleet increased from 672 million tonnes to 1226 million tonnes just over 15 years (1995–2010), see http://ec.europa.eu/transport/ facts-fundings/statistics /doc/2012 /pocketbook2012.pdf
[66]http://www.theguardian.com/environment/2016/may/21/the-worlds-largest-cruise-ship-and-its-supersized-pollution-problem
[67]https://www.transportenvironment.org/what-we-do/shipping/shipping-and-climate-change
[68] *Anthropogenic ocean acidification over the twenty-first century and its impact on calcifying organisms.* J.C Orr e.a. Nature Vol. 437 p. 682.
[69] https://en.wikipedia.org/wiki/Ocean_acidification

Another form of pollution due to an increased world population is noise and light. The number of places in Europe where it is absolutely quiet or pitch-dark at night are decreasing significantly (see Figure 3-11). Almost everywhere you hear road noise or a plane in the air. Light pollution is relatively recent. A recent press article mentions:

"Research indicates that a variety of wildlife behaviours have been significantly altered by night-time light pollution. For example, newly hatched sea turtles crawl inland rather than towards the sea; insects waste their short reproductive lives swarming around street lights; songbirds sing earlier in the year; millions of wild birds die by crashing into lighted structures at night, and migrating birds are increasingly getting lost on their seasonal journeys. In short, wildlife doesn't have to live in or near a city to have their lives disrupted or cut short by city lights."[70]

Figure 3-11: Lights on in Europe (courtesy NASA, DMSP).
Obviously, the light density, recorded in space, correlates very well with population density.

[70]https://www.theguardian.com/science/grrlscientist/2015/aug/26/urban-songbirds-stress-hormones-light-pollution

Climate Change

What was overlooked by the Report for the Club of Rome[71] were the side effects of burning hydrocarbons on the global temperature. Back in 1972, no one foresaw the impact of limitless consumption of hydrocarbons on the Earth's fragile atmosphere. The atmospheric CO_2 concentration is rising sharply because of increased use of fossil fuels but also as a result of a sharply rising world population. In Figure 3-12, the increase in atmospheric CO_2 levels has been approximately split into two effects: the increased energy per capita, largely because of increased economic activity and the rising world population (with an increased energy use).

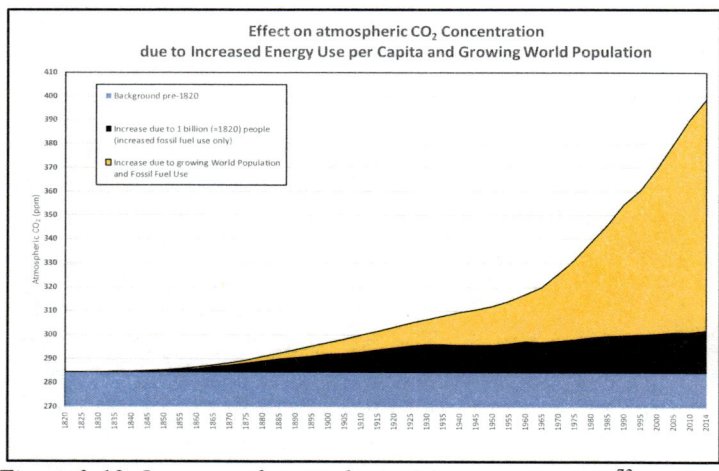

Figure 3-12: Increase of atmospheric CO_2 concentrations[72]

---

[71] *The Limits to Growth:* A report for the Club of Rome Project on the Predicament of Mankind. Dennis L. Meadows ea. (1972)
[72]http://ourworldindata.org/data/resources-energy/energy-production-and-changing-energy-sources/ the curves have been built using historical data of total world energy consumption and world energy consumption per capita, split over four main hydrocarbon categories (biofuels, coal, oil and gas). In producing the black curve, the CO_2 content of different types of hydrocarbons has been weighted differently (gas is producing a lot less). Some CO_2 increase has been catered for from burning biofuels due to permanent deforestation over the last 200 years. Finally, a rough ten-year

What is striking is that the estimated rise in CO_2 levels is largely due to an increased world-population (seven times more than in 1820) and that the effect of increased energy use is relatively minor if the world population is kept at one billion (1820 levels).[73]

Climate change is increasing global temperature and implicitly weather patterns. A hotter planet will have consequences for the habitats of every species, us including. Sea level rise will drown islands and low lying coastal areas in countries like Bangladesh, ironically one of the poorest nations who have had only a minor influence in the global temperature rise. Similarly, very poor countries like Mali and Niger will get even hotter and drier, hitting the poor disproportionately. This will aggravate the exodus, which is already taking place from these countries. It is also estimated that parts of the Persian Gulf will become too hot to live without air-conditioning, spurring potentially more mass movements and arresting further development there.[74]

Since a growing world population is already causing an increased migration, due to more people living below the poverty line, this is only aggravated by climate change-induced migration. This occurs in the poorest countries where climate change hits hardest and where as a result, wars are fought over dwindling natural resources. This is adding pressure to other countries, something which is already clear from recent migration into Europe. Several countries in the developed world are also under threat from expected sea-level rise, caused by warming

delay between burning the hydrocarbons and atmospheric CO_2 increase has been factored in, since the atmospheric dilution effect is not instantaneous.
[73] Implicitly in this assumption is that the increased part of the world population since 1820 (say 6 billion) has on average the same energy consumption pattern as the 1 billion people, responsible for the increased hydrocarbon only. Recently in particular, the added population is mostly located in the poorer countries, using a substantially smaller amount of energy. The shown split due to an increased population might therefore be somewhat smaller. The overall message remains striking however.
[74]http://www.independent.co.uk/news/science/the-countries-that-will-be-so-hot-by-2100-humans-won-t-be-able-to-go-outside-a6710121.html

temperatures, reduction of sediment supply in rivers (due to dams) or from normal compaction (Netherlands, Louisiana[75] in the USA). Maintaining coastal defences requires vast amounts of money.

Efforts are made to limit greenhouse gas emissions, but to solve the problem globalised action is needed. Powerful adversaries exist, such as established industrial corporations, which have much to lose from a reduced hydrocarbon energy consumption, such as coal, oil and gas companies as well as companies making cars, based on combustion engines. They also lobby to weaken governments, maintain an army of legal eagles and have powerful public relation departments to influence the media.[76] These same lobbies are probably behind Trump's surprise election as US president. Not for nothing was he targeting unemployed coal miners and workers in the car industry in the rust belt states.

In principle, however, governments would like to see a drop in Green House Gas (GHG) emissions. The track record of the EU is relatively impressive: emissions in the EU27 GHG emissions dropped from 5589 to 4616 million tonnes CO_2 equivalent over 20-year period 1990–2009. However, after a closer look at the data it was noted that the transport GHG emissions in the EU27 rose from 951 to 1225 million tonnes CO_2 equivalent over the same period.[77] It is expected that the emissions of the EU due to transport will continue to rise in the coming decades as a result of demographic pressures.[78]

The overall drop in GHG emissions in the EU27 is mainly a result of the sharply reduced economic activity in 2009, a continuing conversion of electricity generation by solar and wind power, whilst the overall economic structure of the EU may have shifted to less energy intensive economic activities.[79] It is striking

[75]http://www.theguardian.com/global/commentisfree/2016/may/08/climate-change-refugees-louisiana-rising-seas-vicki-arroyo
[76] Naomi Klein. *This Changes Everything* (2014) Penguin edition p. 173.
[77]http://ec.europa.eu/transport/facts-fundings/statistics/doc/2012/pocketbook2012.pdf
[78]http://ec.europa.eu/eurostat/statistics-explained/index.php/Climate_change_-_driving_forces
[79] Ibid

that manufacturing in Europe is now cleaner due to the use of renewables, nuclear or less polluting gas and increased energy efficiency, whilst we import more manufactured goods from China, produced with high emission coal burning. Conveniently that is off the books in Europe, but overall the global numbers increase.

Now let us leave the popular subject of environmental pressures and return to food security and how we manage affordable and sustainable food production for more than 11 billion people by the end of the century.

Chapter 4
Food and Water Supply and a Different Kind of Economics

"Malthus has been buried many times and Malthusian scarcity with him. But anyone who has to be reburied so often cannot be entirely dead."

—Herman Daly

Can we feed 11 billion people sustainably?

By 2100 the planet is expected to accommodate at least 11 billion people[80] under the most realistic forecast scenario. The agro-business is confident that we can feed the 50% increase in population. But then reflections bubble up on this form of agriculture:

- What type of agriculture do we envisage: industrial style, all organic or a mix?
- How much energy is needed for this?
- Will planetary limits to global warming, pollution and biodiversity be respected or will everything be subordinate to food production?
- What lifestyle are we assuming for every human being? The current dreadful inequality in the world or a fairer one?
- Given planetary constraints, are the rich prepared to live more frugal to accommodate more people in the world?

---

[80]https://www.sciencedaily.com/releases/2015/08/ 1508101 10634.htm

A lot of claims have been made by the industrial agricultural lobby that we can feed the world in the foreseeable future by an increased use of fertiliser, GM crops and more and more industrial-scale farms for cows, pigs and poultry. And even the liberal and green spectrum of the population feels that sustainable agriculture can feed many more mouths. These latter claims are often based on a small number of successful trials extrapolated to world scale applications, whilst ignoring, just to name a few, variations in soil quality and precipitation, reduced crop yield with increased temperatures or socio-political circumstances.

The world's total land area comprises 149 million km^2, but excluding the ice cover it only amounts to some 130 million km^2. Only 49 million km^2 or roughly 38% of the ice-free land mass is considered suitable for agriculture (sum of arable land, permanent crop and meadows/pastures).[81] The rest of the planet consists of forests (31%) and the remaining 31% is not suitable for agriculture (mountains, deserts, tundra, urbanisation and mining),[82] see also Figure 4-1.

Land used for agriculture (cropland or the sum of arable land and permanent crops) does not remain fertile indefinitely. It is subject to degradation and the more intense farming is taking place, the more degraded a soil can become. Degradation is typically caused by water or wind erosion, waterlogging, nutrient mining, salinisation, lowering of the water table and overuse of chemicals. It is estimated that roughly a quarter of the cropland is already suffering decline in quality and productivity but in various degrees. The United Nations Environmental Program (UNEP) has issued a report[83] in early 2014 on how cropland will evolve in the future, based on scenarios of population growth, crop yield and climate change. A self-imposed safe operating space of 16.4 million km^2 (1640 M ha) out of the 49 million km^2, suitable for

---

[81] Fact sheet A04 from FAO, http://faostat3.fao.org/ browse/R/RL/E
[82] http://www.globalchange.umich.edu/globalchange2 /current/lectures/food_supply/food.htm
[83] UNEP (2014) *Assessing Global Land Use: Balancing Consumption with Sustainable Supply*. A Report of the Working Group on Land and Soils of the International Resource Panel. Bringezu S., Schütz H., Pengue W., O´Brien M., Garcia F., Sims R., Howarth R., Kauppi L., Swilling M., and Herrick J. ISBN 978-92-807-3330-3.

agriculture, has been assumed in this report.[84] The safe operating space is a preliminary and indicative value, based on a cautious global target[85] to halt the expansion of global cropland into grasslands, savannahs and forests. In Figure 4-2 a range of estimates for cropland growth is given (blue green lines), as well as a gross growth range by taking assumptions into account for existing cropland degradation,[86,87] needing replacement and for compensation of built-up land on fertile soil (orange lines).

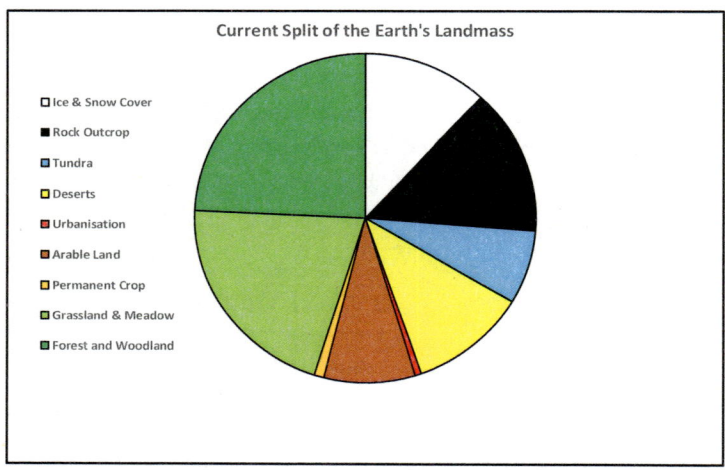

Figure 4-1: Current split of the 149 million km² of the Earth's surface. Roughly a third is suitable for agriculture (sum of arable land, permanent crop and grassland and meadow), but forests and woodlands are under threat.

[84] There is much debate on this. Mark Lynas in his book *The God Species* (2011) quotes 1995 M ha as a limit (p.235), but also this is a self-imposed limit. Lynas number is based on ref. 85.

[85] http://thebreakthrough.org/blog/Planetary%20Boundaries%20web.pdf p. 13 discusses a higher arbitrary target.

[86] More than 1000 Mha is affected by degradation and between 2–5 Mha of cropland is severely degraded every year, see ref. 83.

[87] Some Estimates mention even higher numbers up to 12 M ha annual loss, see http://link.springer.com/article/10.1007%2Fs12571-015-0437-x#page-1

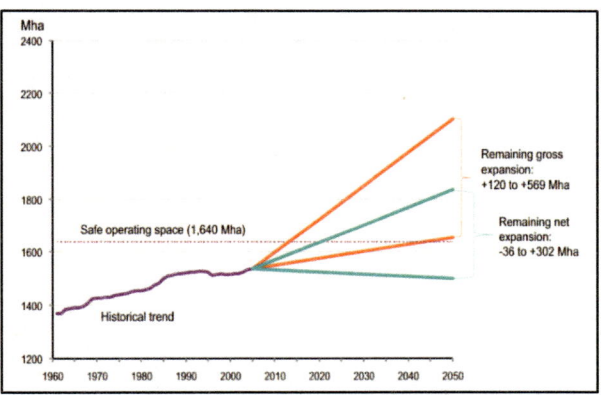

Figure 4-2: Forecasted evolution of global cropland (arable land plus permanent crop) until 2050 in million ha. This <u>includes</u> 'land saving' measures (i.e. not 'business as usual'), such as better planning, control, diet and less soil degradation. A range is given for these net estimates, whilst gross estimates include assumptions on existing cropland degradation, needing replacement and on compensation for built-up land on fertile soil.[88]

As can be seen from Figure 4-2, the range in gross cropland expansion estimates will exceed the safe operating space between now and 2050, even when taking 'land saving' measures into account. The range of estimates increases dramatically under a 'business as usual' scenario. This does not bode well for the remaining forest and grassland habitats. As the UNEP report states *'the challenge for policy change is enormous'.*[89]

Whilst land use (and indirectly biodiversity) is expected to be under pressure from human population growth, the crop yield is expected to rise due to efficiency improvements and future innovations. This has been addressed in the UNEP report, which is based on estimates from J. Bruinsma (2009).[90] The increase over time is levelling off however, see Figure 4-3. Also, crop yield is expected to be affected by climate change, although it is

---

[88] Ref. 83 pages 13–15.

[89] Ibid p 92.

[90] ftp://ftp.fao.org/agl/aglw/docs/ResourceOutlookto2050.pdf

uncertain in which direction, due to potential positive effects of CO_2 fertilisation .[91]

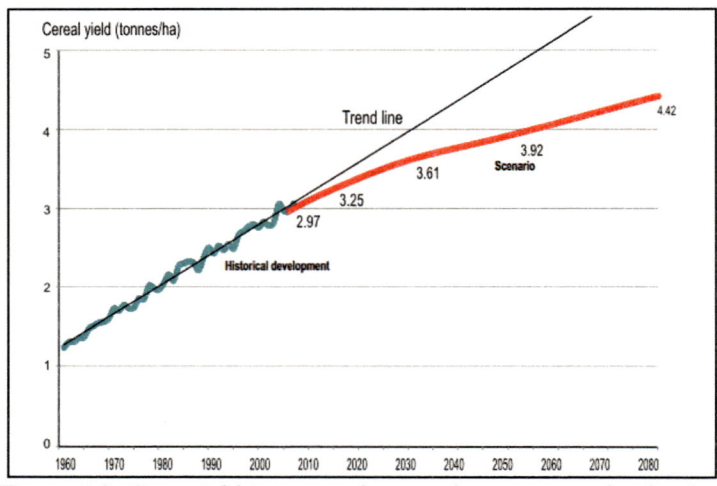

Figure 4-3: Crop yield increases for cereals are expected to level off over time[92]

Of the 49 million km^2 of land, suitable for agriculture, currently only 0.44 million km^2 (or less than 1%) is applying organic farming.[93] We are by no means ready to replace traditional and large scale industrial farming by organic farming practices. Not only that, but there are conflicting evidences about crop yield of organic farming. Both the industrial agricultural lobby as organic farming organisations quote a large variation of numbers. A literature study conducted in 2012 indicated that, based on 362 publications, the organic yields of individual crops are on average 80% of conventional yields but variation is substantial (standard

---

[91] http://www.fao.org/3/a-ak972e.pdf Table 5.2

[92] Ref. 83 Figure 3.1

[93] End 2014 data from http://www.fibl.org/en/media/media-archive/media-archive16/media-release15/article/bio-waechst-weiter-weltweit-437-millionen-hektar-bioflaeche.html

deviation 21%).[94] Many studies show an even narrower gap.[95] Sustainable farming (or more scientifically known as agroecology) avoids monocultures (organic or not), uses intercropping and crop rotations and mixes live-stock with traditional food production. Crop yield gains over the last 10 years in Sub-Saharan Africa and Latin America seem impressive,[96] but similar gains need to be extended over the next 50 years to feed the expected additional population. It is unclear whether the agroecological experiments are representative for up-scaling purposes. In the meantime, however, it is noticed that monocultures at an industrial scale can be vulnerable for some fungal diseases (e.g. stem rust in wheat varieties), threatening food supply in sub-Saharan Africa.

Current crop yield also depends on the use of nitrogen fertiliser. Every year we are converting 121 million tonnes of atmospheric nitrogen into fertilisers.[97] This is causing pollution on a large scale (loss of biodiversity, algal blooms and corresponding oceanic death zones). A safe limit of 35 million tonnes is mentioned (more than 3.5 times less than the current yearly use), based on ref. 85, p.19, but the reference limit seems to be chosen arbitrarily. The large-scale environmental impact of fertiliser use (both phosphor and nitrogen) remains unknown. Setting artificial limits does not help and since we are already over these, this allows needless leniency for potential environmental degradation.[98] Mark Lynas believes in the solution of genetically manipulated (GM) crops, allowing for more nitrogen efficient plants, which could drastically reduce fertiliser use.[99] However, five years after Lynas' book there are still no fertiliser-frugal transgenic crops on the market.[100]

---

[94] *The crop yield gap between organic and conventional agriculture.* Tonnek de Ponti ea. Agricultural Systems Vol. 108, April 2012, Pages 1–9.
[95] http://www.worldwatch.org/node/4060
[96]http://uk.reuters.com/article/us-food-idUKTRE7272FN20110308
[97] *The God Species* by Mark Lynas (2011). Fourth Estate books p. 235.
[98]http://www.nature.com/climate/2009/0910/full/climate.2009.93.html
99 *The God Species* by Mark Lynas (2011). Fourth Estate books p. 100-109.
100 http://www.nature.com/news/the-race-to-create-super-crops-1.19943

And How about Water?

Today 36% of the global population lives in water-scarce regions. If we do nothing, by 2050 this will increase to 50%.[101] Water scarcity can be split up in physical water scarcity and economic water scarcity. The latter is solely related to the affordability of water by the population. There are three important concepts to water availability:

- The first concept is sustainability, since water withdrawals need to be offset by recharging. Currently most of the North African and Middle Eastern countries have unsustainable water withdrawals. In the long run this will affect food production as well, something which has hardly entered the projections of future crop yields. Rich countries in the Persian Gulf are topping up their water needs by desalination plants and Saudi Arabia's long-term goal is to provide enough solar energy to power all their desalination plants.

- The second important concept is water variability, which is entirely driven by climates. The uncertainty in future precipitation related to climate change is probably the most important factor driving future water scarcity. Various climatic models predict differences in precipitation. In particular, Central America, Southern Europe and Southern Africa could experience lower precipitations. Receding glaciers with global warming is another concern: Lima in Peru (9 million inhabitants) and northern India/Pakistan and Nepal are at risk of a much-reduced water supply in the future.[102]

- The last concept is water quality. Water quality standards are strongly correlated with prosperity. It comes as no surprise that the poorest countries in the world have the poorest quality water, since it is there where economic water scarcity is highest. Not only that, but the poorest

---

101 http://growingblue.com/implications-of-growth/social-implications/
[102] *Adventures in the Anthropocene*, Gaia Vince (2014). Vintage Pocket Edition.

countries also have the highest fertility rate, causing even more clean water stress in the future.

Water scarcity and population pressure are likely inputs to conflicts, wars and migrations. The damming of water of the Euphrates and Tigris in Turkey reduced the water flow to Syria by 40% and to Iraq by 80% since 1975,[103] causing accusations and a potential for conflict. In Syria, a drought in 2006 caused migration of desolate and disgruntled farmers to city centres, triggering instability because of unemployment. The consequent war and migration are like domino-stones in this much bigger picture.

More People, More Jobs?

From the preceding sections, it is clear that food and water may become scarcer in the future, not in the least because we are with more people. Apart from ecological considerations such as sustainability, the other important consideration is whether our food and clean water are affordable. Before tackling economics, let's talk about the future money supply in a world of rapidly expanding population.

Future population growth will take place predominantly in the poorer parts of the world, due to a strong link between poverty and fertility (see Figure 4-4). It comes as no surprise that unemployment is higher in poorer countries and even higher than officially recorded.[104] A lot of people in the developing countries could be 'employed' but in inefficient and non-automated public services, whilst many women in traditional societies are not counted as unemployed since they are not allowed to work outdoors.

---

[103] http://www.smithsonianmag.com/innovation/is-a-lack-of-water-to-blame-for-the-conflict-in-syria-72513729/?no-ist

[104] For that reason, I am not detailing it here. There are some numbers by country around, but estimates are from different years: https://www.cia.gov/library/publications/the-world-factbook/rankorder/2129rank.html

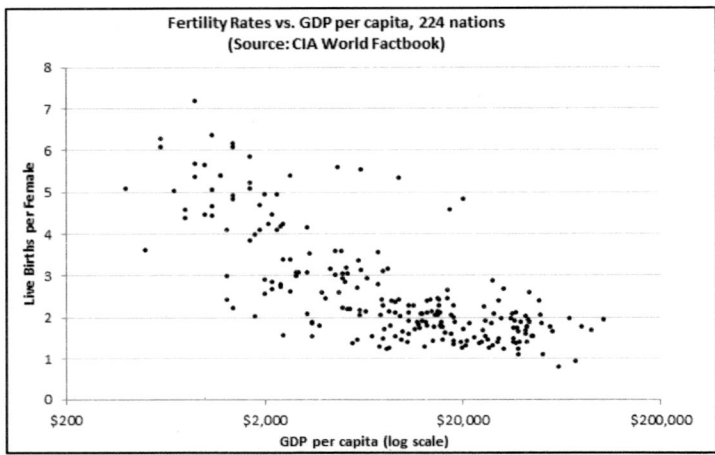

Figure 4-4: The poorer the country, the higher the fertility

Poverty and unemployment are the main driving forces for economic migration. The four billion additional people by the end of the century will be predominantly located in the poorer parts of the world (Africa on its own will generate already more than three billion extra people by 2100, according to the latest UN estimates),[105] where unemployment is already high.

In general, employment opportunities do not keep up linearly with population growth. When population rises by 10%, one does not need 10% more road building or 10% more trains. The consequences are that with increasing population, unemployment as a percentage will rise. Of course, the employment rate is influenced by other factors such as natural disasters, diseases, wars, hunger and financial crises. The more modern threat to employment is automation, rationalisation and the introduction of robots. This is only just kicking off in a serious manner. Of course, it is a good thing that menial work (such as conveyer belt work) is reducing and being done by machines, but there is a careful balance between the meaning of having a job (and income) and not having a meaningful job. Recent research suggests that 47%

---

[105] https://esa.un.org/unpd/wpp/DataQuery/ accessed 22 June 2016.

of the jobs in the US are at risk of being automated in the next 20 years.[106] My suspicion is that faster automation of meaningless jobs is held back by fear of rising unemployment.

Yuval Harari mentions in his book *Homo Deus* several examples of jobs, which could disappear in the near future.[107] Medical Artificial Intelligence (e.g. IBM's Watson programme) will reduce the need for doctors, whilst automated cars (e.g. Google's and Tesla's efforts) will eventually replace most of our driving. Despite what has been predicted earlier (see p. 322 of Harari's book), truck drivers could soon be a thing of the past. These replacements are not only economically driven but also from a safety standpoint. Tram or train drivers falling asleep at the wheel are more prone to accidents than a fully automated system. Inexperience or just a bad day of a doctor could have serious health consequences for a patient. When given the choice, people will soon prefer driverless transport or rely on a vast data base for medical problems. Moreover, the human investment in training every new doctor from scratch with the full history and latest developments of the medical science, does not seem very efficient.

With automation looming, the old idea of a Universal Basic Income (UBI), without any conditions attached, is popping up again.[108] This could go hand in hand with progressive automation and rationalisation, resulting in a smaller amount of jobs and thus giving more time to devote to our true interests. A UBI also promotes more equality and due to its simplicity, a more efficient administration is claimed which is less prone to fraud. Unemployment benefits and pensions could be replaced by a UBI, although old age may not be the same for everybody and some people need more or earlier care than others.

Calculations show that the introduction of a UBI is economically feasible without any additional costs, as a

---

[106]http://www.eng.ox.ac.uk/about/news/new-study-shows-nearly-half-of-us-jobs-at-risk-of-computerisation
[107] *Homo Deus: A Brief History of Tomorrow.* Chapter 9. Y. Harari. Harvill Secker (2016)
[108] *The Immaterial*, André Gorz (2010), Seagull Books

consultation paper of the UK's Green Party suggests.[109] However other sources disagree: in a June 2016 referendum in Switzerland, 23% of the population agreed with the introduction of a basic income, but the main parties in Switzerland suggest that its introduction would cost an extra 25 billion Swiss Francs per year.[110] There continues to be significant interest in the subject with pilot schemes planned in Finland, the Netherlands and the US,[111] countries where technological advances are progressing fast. The key thing is that the scheme promotes more equality, which is unfortunately not supported by most people, since an increased equality is a truly Marxist concept. Another premise for the idea of a basic income is that the population in a country needs to remain more or less constant. Dramatic increases in births, immigration or a decreasing amount of deaths would strain this idea significantly.

A Different Kind of Economics

"The rapid growth of the last 200 years has occurred because man broke the budget constraint of living on solar income and began to live on geological capital."[112]

The '*breaking of the budget constraint*' in the above quotation sounds like Prometheus playing with fire and invoking the wrath of the Gods. It is realised that using fossil fuel as a basis for our energy needs, is causing irreparable damage to our climate and ultimately, we cannot avoid perishing (see discussion on Climate Change in the previous chapter). But also, other natural resources such as wood and valuable ores are part of the '*geological capital*'. These may not be as finite as suggested by report for the

---

[109]https://policy.greenparty.org.uk/assets/files/Policy%20files/Basic%20Income%20Consultation%20Paper.pdf

[110]http://www.nytimes.com/2016/06/06/world/europe/switzerland-swiss-vote-basic-income.html?_r=0

[111]https://www.theguardian.com/technology/2016/jun/22/silicon-valley-universal-basic-income-y-combinator

[112] *Steady State Economics* – Herman Daly. Second Edition (1991), Island Press. Page 23.

Club of Rome back in 1972,[113] but for some of them[114] we are now beginning to see the bottom of the chest. For other ores (e.g. Coltan in the DRC or 'blood' diamonds in several African countries) human and environmental conditions to mine them are terrible and not sustainable on the long run. Not only that but mining and subsequent refining of ores is very energy intensive; within the OECD countries around 17% of the energy consumption of the industrial sector goes to the mining sector, see Figure 4-5 (sum of iron, steel, non-ferrous metals and non-metallic minerals). For non-OECD countries, the number exceeds currently 25% but is expected to decline in the future.

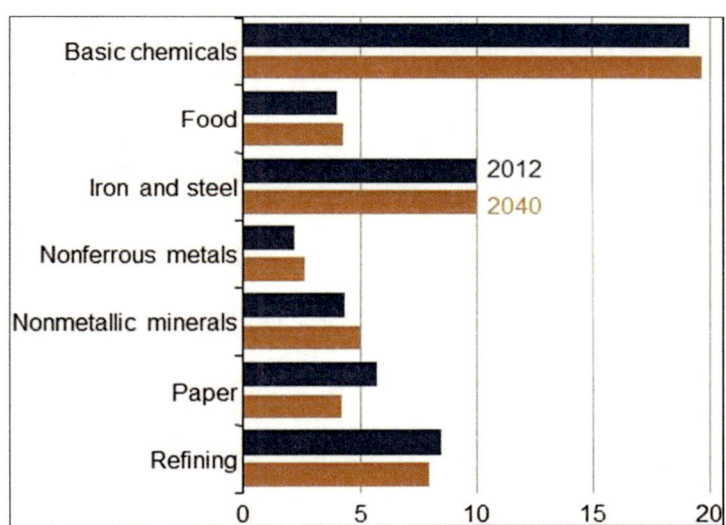

Figure 4-5: Current and Future split of Energy Consumption (%) in the Industrial Sector of OECD countries[115]

[113] *The Limits to Growth* – A report for the Club of Rome Project on the Predicament of Mankind. Dennis L. Meadows ea. (1972)
[114] E.g. Antimony, Molybdenum and Zinc, see *Mineral Resources: Geological Scarcity, Market Price Trends and Future Generations.* Henckens ea. Resource Policies 49 (2016) p. 102–111
[115] http://www.eia.gov/forecasts/ieo/industrial.cfm May 2016.

Now suppose we conquered our dirty habits by extracting all our energy from renewables (wind and solar). Does this mean we get a carte blanche to increase the population without limits? Under that scenario, we may be able to stop increases of atmospheric CO_2, but it would not stop our cities, roads, arable land and mines to sprawl out of control and cause havoc on the environment. Clearly there are other limits than atmospheric CO_2 content.

Economic growth is a strange concept and considered sacrosanct for many. It relies heavily on a bountiful supply of energy, food, water and other resources and is therefore inherently unsteady state. To keep an economy in steady state conditions, it is necessary to keep the following points within limits:[116]

i.   The depletion of energy, materials
ii.   The human population
iii. The degree of inequality

In the true sense of steady state, the first point would promote the use of renewable energy rather than fossil fuels, whilst to keep depletion of materials within check, recycling should be heavily promoted. Herman Daly even quotes that inequality is initially promoted by economic growth,[117] but the reverse statement, that inequality ultimately hampers economic growth, is reasonably well accepted these days.[118] As stated in Chapter 2, the concept of inequality is strongly related to population growth as well and the same interrelatedness is noted: inequality causes population growth and population growth is a cause for inequality.

In his book, Daly quotes several incentives to get towards a steady state economy. One of them is capping the distribution of wealth by putting limits to the minimum salary (essentially a basic income) as well as a maximum limit (five times the average

---

[116] Loosely after H. Daly, *Steady State Economics*, Island Press, second edition (1991), p.53.

[117] H. Daly, *Steady State Economics*, Island Press, second edition (1991), p.44.

[118]http://www.economist.com/news/finance-and-economics/21597931-up-point-redistributing-income-fight-inequality-can-lift-growth-inequality

income). The other incentive to get us to a steady state economy, is introducing a quota-based system for non-renewable materials. For the third pre-requisite of a steady state economy, Daly suggests controlling the population growth by a rather crude tradable point system,[119] which seems very outdated and not effective.

More recent views express that organisational changes are needed for the concept of economic well-being, since an economy dominated by shareholders who only take a stake in firms to make a quick profit without any longer-term commitment, is driven relentlessly to growth.[120]

We are currently experiencing very low or zero growth in the western world due to the 2008/2009 financial crisis. Economies do not come to a complete standstill; however, in some countries a declining population can offset a negative GDP growth. For example, Japan is still managing a GDP growth on a per capita basis. This phenomenon is also visible from a PWC study, conducted in February 2015 (see Figure 4-6). I am rather sceptical on the GDP growth predictions for Nigeria (first bar in Figure 4-6): on average, more than 5% annual growth of GDP per capita seems unrealistic when the population is growing by 2.5% annually causing, even now, a sizeable diaspora to European countries.

Before leaving this section on economics, some words are needed on the costs of overpopulation. There are some clear advantages of living in a town or city, in particular the aspect of economy of scale. Therefore, shopping and transport are much cheaper or easier within cities compared to the countryside: a lot of distance can be covered on foot, whilst bus/underground services are relatively cheap. Housing is generally less spacious and more expensive in cities. When a city becomes bigger and bigger, house prices are increasing and consequently the lower earners are displaced towards the suburbs. In the extreme case, house prices could sky-rocket even further in mega-cities, such as

---

[119] H. Daly, *Steady State Economics*, Island Press, second edition, Chapter 3.

[120] http://www.neweconomics.org/blog/entry/policies-for-a-zero-growth-economy

London, due to lax regulation on foreign ownership (city moguls, oil barons, kleptocratic oligarchs or mafia). Not only pay these privileged a fortune for their housing, but also essential workers, such as hospital nurses and teachers, need to be supported to allow them to live near the places where they provide their services.

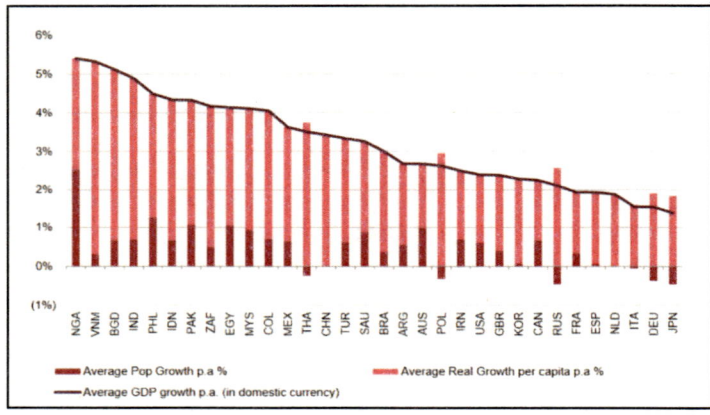

*Figure 4-6: Average annual growth of Population, GDP per capita and ranked by GDP over period **2014–2050** for a select number of countries.[121] Note that countries with expected declining populations (Thailand, Poland, Russia, Germany and Japan) have an average GDP per capita growth above the trend.*

When a city continues to sprawl, a lot more infrastructure is needed. But this again attracts more people and traffic jams and other forms of congestion are taking their toll on both human costs (less quality time left and extra costs, such a parking fees) as well as costs to business. In 2013 the business costs of congestion alone amounted to $200 million in four countries (USA, UK, France and Germany) or 0.8% of their GDP. Two-thirds of the costs incurred are the result of wasted fuel and time that could be better spent elsewhere, and the remainder from increased business expenses.[122] With expected increases in the number of cars, this

[121]https://www.pwc.com/gx/en/issues/the-economy/assets/world-in-2050-february-2015.pdf

[122]http://www.economist.com/blogs/economist-explains/2014/11/economist

number is expected to rise to $300 million by 2030. These costs are only the costs for the four countries, mentioned above and are only related to increased traffic. The cost of extra regulation (e.g. fines for speeding, fees for parking), accidents (more impact in densely populated areas) or air pollution and its resulting health costs will only increase these amounts.

Chapter 5
Culture, Religion and Anti-Conception

Culture

"Don't blame me for my six children, we have a different culture."
—Answer from a young Nigerian father

Arguments like this are commonplace, but do they hold? Just replace '*my six children*' by '*wife beating*', the '*Death Sentence*' or '*FGM*', and one gets the message: do not interfere with me, we are just different. Respect for differences in cultures is a noble thing, but are there no limits?

In addition to poverty and consequent poor or absent education, 'culture' is a main driving force for high fertility rates as well. As can be seen in Figure 5-1, high fertility rates are predominantly occurring in African countries.

One of the cultural driving forces for high fertility in Africa is male infidelity, which probably has deep roots in polygyny: out of 39 countries around the world, African countries take up 25 slots on the rankings where men have children with multiple women[123] (see also Figure 5-2). These multiple-women fathers include polygynous men, married men who cheat on their partners and unmarried men in sexual relationships with different women.

---

[123] *State of the World's Fathers* by R. Levtov, N. van der Gaag, M. Greene, M. Kaufman and G. Barker (2015). A MenCare Advocacy Publication. Washington, DC. Promundo, Rutgers, Save the Children, Sonke Gender Justice, and the MenEngage Alliance. Also via http://sowf.s3. Amazonaws.com/wp-content/uploads/2015/06/08181421/State-of-the-Worlds-Fathers_23June2015.pdf

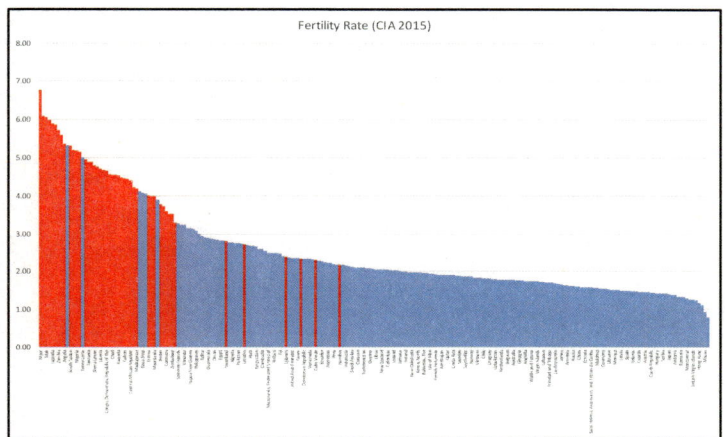
Figure 5-1: Fertility rate ranked by country. In red are African countries. Data from CIA (2015)[124]

As we shall see in Chapter 7, these families with multiple fathers are not the most stable ones for the children and consequently put immense pressures on the mother. If we want to eradicate high fertility in Africa, we must not only address poverty and educate women but educate men as well, to change their sexual behaviour or cultural prejudice.

Initiatives are taking place to involve fathers into more care for their children or to urge them to use less violence at home. It is also noticed that nuclear families are increasing to supply a globalised world with maximum employment flexibility anywhere. Consequently, extended families are decreasing and thus the role of a second caretaker is becoming more important[125].

[124]https://www.cia.gov/library/publications/the-world-factbook/rankorder/2127rank.html
[125] Ibid.

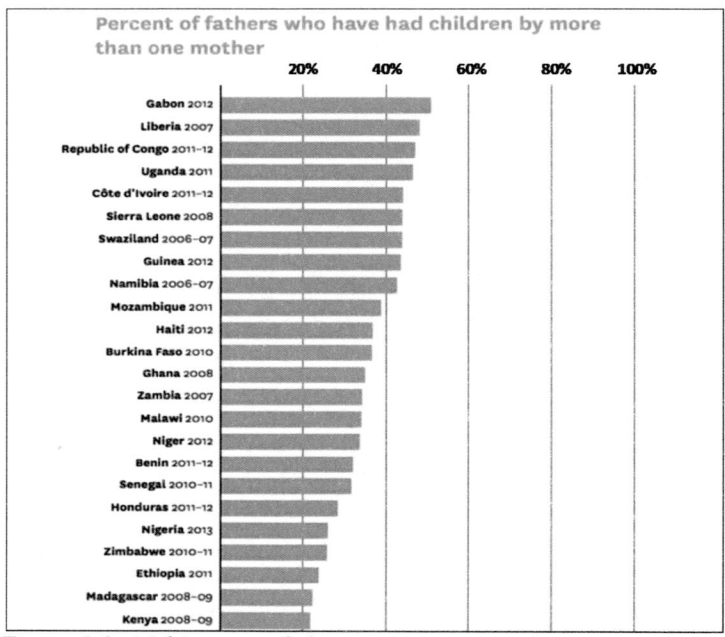

Figure 5-2: Multi-women fathers are a common phenomenon in Africa[126]

Extended families are more common in Southern Europe, Latin America, Asia and Africa. Despite disadvantages, such as more prevalent abuse (see Chapter 7), extended families seem overall better for the child's stability and upbringing. A demographic side-effect of extended families is that it also affects the fertility rate positively. In the developed countries family planning is done more frequently in a nuclear family, for the wrong reasons however: when both parents work (no time left to raise children...) or in very poor nuclear families (no money, no fall-back to extended family).

Also, gender-bias can be a reason for a higher fertility in cultures, which value boys more than girls: it is more likely that a couple will continue to extend the family size if there are so far

---

[126] Ibid., Figure 3-2.

only girls born. And these stories are not limited to developing countries, such as India. I have personally experienced a gender-biased farmer in the Netherlands, who opted for the extra child, since the first two were girls, who were not considered 'suitable' to continue the farm business and who would lose their family name upon marriage.

Cultures are also responsible for the suppression of women. In the developing world, girls are considered not needing as much education as boys. Instead, money for education of a girl or young woman is saved for a dowry. On the receiving end, dowries are used as a survival strategy: with the dowry, cattle are bought or exchanged, which is vital to feed the large family. Moreover, in some countries the education of a girl is increasing the price of the dowry, which in turn would incentivise the family into early marriage.[127] In countries where school fees are high, a young girl might be promised to an older man, who would in turn foot the bill for her education.[128] These examples show that the development of women is commodified in a patriarchal culture by dowries or educational exchanges to cover up disproportionate difference in age and a slave-like dependency in later life.

The ability to sire many children (in or outside wedlock) is still seen in many cultures as a sign of male strength (still lingering in the west as well, remember the saying 'I am man enough to fill a pram'). People look up at these men with a sense of awe and respect (Genghis Khan is known to hold the record having fathered between 6000 and 8000 children). This patriarchal culture goes often hand in hand with an obsessive (and hypocritical!) reverence for female virginity. It has its roots in male fertility folklore of the Hindi or Greek Gods of yore (Zeus is infamous for his erotic escapes and his many children). In the world of today, it seems mindlessly animalistic to emphasise the number of progeny and thus ignoring the fact that we are members of a social species, who have responsibilities towards each other. Modern humans should care more about the total species than focussing on individual achievements.

---

[127] *How Population Change Will Transform Our World.* Sarah Harper (2016). Oxford University Press. p.131
[128] Ibid. p. 131

Women in sub-Saharan Africa sometimes express a desire to have a large offspring as well, albeit generally a smaller amount than their husbands. Sarah Harper wonders whether this is *'embedded in the culture of sub-Saharan Africa'.[129]* I think this is resulting from indoctrination of patriarchal cultures: keeping the women poorly educated, fully dependent on the husband and his family and rarely leaving the village. Ignorance and fear probably lay at the basis of these opinions, not a genuine desire of another culture.

Fortunately, cultures are dynamic; it is not forever. Outdated concepts of a culture generally disappear (i.e. cannibalism by Papua New Guinea tribes is no longer taking place, lively discussions in Egypt to abolish FGM[130] or the 'Black Pete' discussions in the Netherlands).[131] To shame, blame and ban 'accepted' male infidelity or polygyny in Africa produces a triple whammy: it liberates African women from a miserable existence; it will reduce the fertility rate and will consequently give children some real parenting. It is good to break the norm of an established culture.

A Right to Reproduce?

Reproductive rights are part of the human rights. The decision on the number of children is considered a human right as well, but important provisos and themes seem to change as times go by, once emancipation in the 1960s kicked off. Here are a number of statements[132] with changing provisos (my underlining and bolding):

---

[129] Ibid. p. 54

[130] With not much success so far, however.
https://www.theguardian.com/world/2015/feb/06/female-genital-mutilation-egypt

[131] http://www.telegraph.co.uk/news/worldnews/europe/netherlands/119965 88/Dutch-Black-Pete-makes-annual-arrival-to-howls-of-protest.html

[132] http://www.un.org/en/development/desa/population/theme/rights/

*"The majority of parents desire to have the knowledge and the means a plan their families; that the opportunities to decide <u>the number</u> and spacing <u>of children</u> is a **basic human right**."*

Human Rights Day, 10 December 1966, Declaration on Population.

*"The Universal Declaration of Human Rights describes the family as the natural and fundamental unit of society. It follows that any choice and decision <u>with regard to the size of the family must inevitably rest with the family itself</u>, and cannot be made by anyone else. **But this right of parents to free choice will remain illusory unless they are aware of the alternatives open to them.** Hence, the right of every family to information and the availability of services in the field is increasingly considered as a basic human right and as an indispensable ingredient of human dignity."*

Human Rights Day, 10 December 1967

*It affirmed the Tehran Proclamation and urged Governments to provide couples not only the 'education' but also the 'means necessary to enable them to exercise their right to determine freely and **responsibly** <u>the number</u> and spacing <u>of their children</u>'.*

1969 Declaration on Social Progress and Development, resolution 2542, UN Doc. A/7630

*Reproductive rights in WPPA: "All couples and individuals have the basic right to decide freely and **responsibly** <u>the number</u> and spacing <u>of their children</u> and to **have the information, education and means to do so; the responsibility of couples** and individuals in the exercise of this right **takes into account the needs of their living and future** children, **and their responsibilities toward the community."**

World Population Plan of Action (WPPA, para 14(f) in Principles and Objectives)

"...reproductive rights embrace certain human rights that are already recognised in national laws, international human rights documents and other relevant United Nations consensus documents. These rights rest on the recognition of the basic right

*of all couples and individuals to decide freely and **responsibly** the number, spacing and timing of their children and to **have the information and means to do so**, and the right to attain the highest standard of sexual and reproductive health. It also includes the right of all **to make decisions concerning reproduction free of discrimination, coercion and violence** as expressed in human rights documents. In the exercise of this right, they should take into account the needs of their living and future children and their responsibilities towards the community."*
(ICPD Programme of Action 1994, para 7.3)

The 1994 International Conference on Population and Development (ICPD) in Cairo

What is clear from the above attempts to use provisos that reproductive decisions should be made well-informed, freely and responsibly? I cannot agree more. However pragmatically none of these conditions seem to be met in countries with high fertility rate: people are not free in their decision-making on reproductive matters due to very strong cultural, religious or financial pressures, which also prevent people to make well-informed or responsible decisions, free of bias.

And what is well-informed? Outside one's culture, it is difficult to make sensible decisions on the number of children, since one is unaware of the bigger picture. That bigger picture is important, since we live increasingly in a globalised world: what happens in an African country with an isolated culture has repercussions for the rest of the world (e.g. migrations due to over-population), as well as vice versa (e.g. climate change, predominantly caused by developed nations).

I often compare the right to reproduce with the right to smoke in the western world. Yes, people have a right to smoke, but not in public places, where passive smoking of non-smokers can cause unwanted lung-cancer. Hence there are rules: please smoke outside or in dedicated rooms. People can reproduce themselves, but the problem of a growing world population is crying out for, in the words of the Human Right Declarations, "*responsible decisions.*" A fast-growing world population is causing environmental pressures, traffic jams, crowded schools and financial uncertainty for everybody. Limits need to be drawn on the number of children, one decides to have. It is time this gets embedded in reproductive rights statements, free from cultural or religious bias. In an increasingly globalised world, it is impossible to take account of everybody's wishes. The result would be chaos.

Religion

This book is written with atheists in mind. Religious discussions involving God and books more than 1000 years old on what is allowed and not allowed in the current modern world with global warming and other planetary limits, seem ludicrous.

In religious debates, the right to live of unborn human beings seems to take precedence over the wellbeing of the people in existence, who have rights too (see various articles in the Universal Declaration of Human Rights). For many people, their Human Rights are violated on a daily basis: is it therefore not more ethical that the rights of people already born should take precedence over the unborn? The argument that the unborn cannot respond, is not an exclusive argument to the unborn. A large part of the human population lives in abject poverty, in war zones or in situations of modern slavery and their voices are unfortunately (or deliberately?) not always heard.

In any case, killing unborn life (abortion) should be a last resort. Contraception as a means to limit the world population is also met with resistance by religious leaders. The Catholic Church is still vehemently against any form of contraception, bar abstinence. The reasoning is that artificial contraceptive means are considered '*intrinsically disordered*' because of the belief that all licit sexual acts must be both unitive (express love) *and* procreative.[133] Some Christian groups consider contraception outside the marriage boundary as an encouragement to promiscuity. Other Christian religions are less outspoken on contraception and allow it overtly or covertly.

Islam and Hinduism have no official ban on birth control. Islam is encouraging procreation, but allows contraceptive

---

[133]http://www.nfpandmore.org/Marriage%20Act%20Unitive%20and%20Pr ocreative.pdf

methods to be used as long as it will not cause permanent sterility and not harm the body. It is true that countries with large Muslim populations have dropped their fertility rate significantly over the last 30 years (see Figure 5-3). However, Islam allows polygamy, only with the defence that *'standards of morality are not set by prevalent Western thought, but by divine revelation'*.[134] In other words, do not think, do not progress, just accept God's word ad infinitum. And it is this condoning of archaic habits which perpetuates, amongst others, high fertility rates.

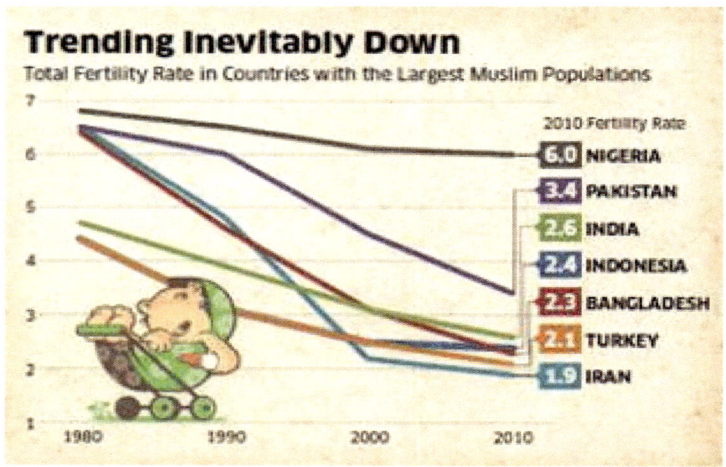

Figure 5-3: Fertility Rate drop for countries with a large Muslim population[135]

Catholicism in particular has left its imprint on several laws and regulations in Southern Europe. The 'Famille Nombreuse' in France or the 'Gran Familia' in Spain still benefit from all kinds of discounts (restaurants, shops, train travel), which seem otherworldly in Northern Europe. The irony is that the Catholic families in those countries no longer count as big and that the

[134]http://www.islamreligion.com/articles/325/an-introduction-to-polygamy-in-islam
[135]http://blogs.timesofindia.indiatimes.com/cursor/muslim-population-myths/

discounts go to poor big Muslim African families instead, probably not what the Catholic Church envisaged!

The promotion of procreation has always had a selfish and cynical streak in the Catholic Church as well. It provided the much-needed labour force to allow the clergy a luxurious life. Without a large proletariat, no cathedral would have been built either. The continuation of a large cheap workforce worked in their advantage and in the advantage of other ruling elites (first aristocracy and later factory owners). The clergy has conspired with the ruling elite on this almost to this very day.

And finally, it is not just religion promoting procreation. Religion has part of its roots in the belief of supernatural causality (superstition). Other brands of superstition (e.g. astrology) can be strong promoters of procreation and this is still quite prevalent in countries with high fertility rates.

Contraception and Education

In the modern world of today contraception has found its place amongst the majority of the population. However, there are still large differences between various regions. A recent UN study[136] indicates that the lack of contraceptive use amongst women is strongly linked to countries where either culture or religion prevail (see Figure 5-4).

People in these countries do not so much quote (or do not dare to quote…) religion or culture as reasons for the limited use of contraception. Rather they quote infrequent sex and concerns regarding side effects or health risks. It is well known that expanding access to contraceptive supplies and services is not sufficient on its own to satisfy demand for family planning. The study quotes that it is more crucial to provide information and counselling to users about all the available contraceptive methods: how to use them, support for switching methods if needed, as well as expanding the range of available modern methods. This is particularly true in poverty stricken areas, where ignorance and superstition are still high. Rather than sending plane loads of

---

[136]http://www.un.org/en/development/desa/population/publications/pdf/family/trendsContraceptiveUse2015Report.pdf

contraceptives it is probably wiser to educate using local family planning nurses.

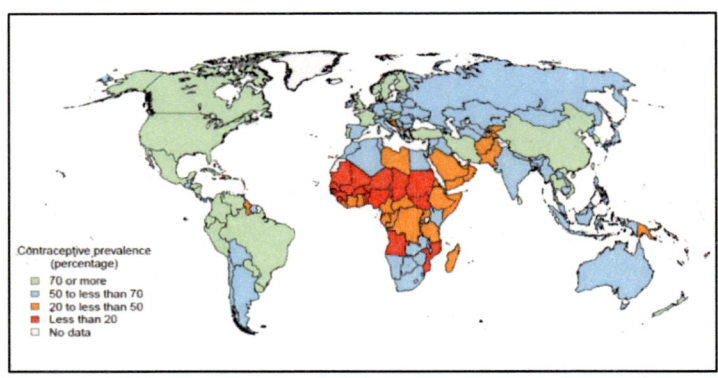

Figure 5-4: There is a strong link between regions where culture and religion prevail and the prevalence of contraceptives (use amongst women 15–49 years, 2015)[137]

Despite cultural and religious bias, people in these areas feel their needs for family planning are not fully met, which implicitly means people really do not want to have so many children. A United Nations study mentions unmet contraceptive needs in some West African countries exceeding 30%.[138] Figure 5-5 highlights these differences for several regions by comparing unmet needs versus contraceptive prevalence between 1970 and 2015. Areas such as West and Middle Africa clearly lag behind the rest of the world.

---

[137] Ibid, Figure 4
[138] Ibid, Figure 5

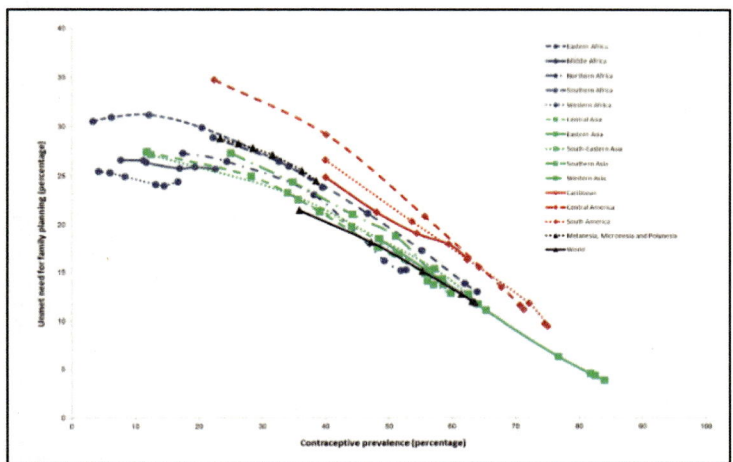

Figure 5-5: Unmet need for family planning versus contraceptive prevalence. Trends from 1970 (leftmost point) to 2015 (rightmost point). Women 15–49 years. Note the sluggish trend for Middle and Western Africa.[139]

Another interesting graph from this study (Figure 5-6) splits the contraceptive use into various methods. In Africa, the contraceptive use is not only low in comparison with the rest of the world, but also the proportion of permanent methods (sterilisation) is lower. Taboos and superstition with roots in culture, are at the base of this and there is still a lot to learn. When it comes to sterilisation it is interesting to note that vasectomy seems completely absent in Africa but is also low in Asia and Latin America, where female sterilisation is more commonplace. Note that in India it is the women who think that vasectomy will leave their husband unable to earn a living, since vasectomy is feared to lose a man's strength and virility.[140] Despite a much more invasive operation, female sterilisation is more socially

---

[139] Reference 136, Figure 7
[140] http://blogs.wsj.com/indiarealtime/2014/11/13/delhis-mega-vasectomy-camp-and-why-indian-men-dont-get-sterilized/

acceptable in India. Unfortunately taboos and superstition still play a too important role.

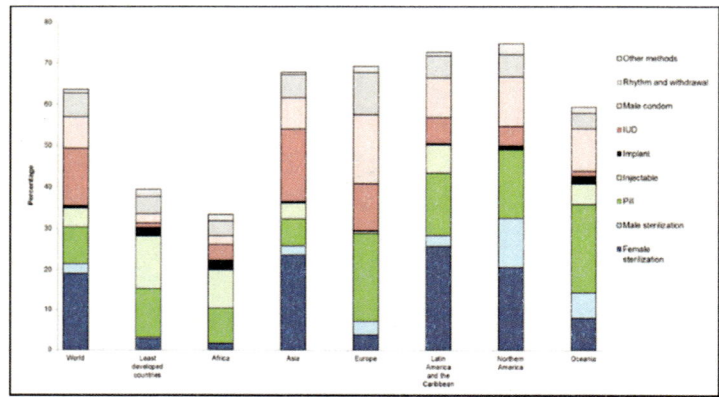

Figure 5-6: Contraceptive prevalence per region. Note the low contraceptive prevalence in Africa with low occurrence of female sterilisation and absence of male sterilisation.[141]

Again, these examples highlight the importance of education. A lot of emphasis has been placed on education, although the cycle of poverty is particularly hard to break. It is often assumed that only developmental aid towards the Third World coupled with aggressive promotion of birth control will eventually cause the population to stabilise.[142] Too often these programmes fail because of corruption and cash is channelled away to a wealthy few, who in turn launder their money in London and its tax havens. Poverty is not eradicated with these programmes and the people are left uneducated.

Of course, there are exceptions: Algeria for example has a much higher enrolment of women in university (36% compared to 25% for men in 2009).[143] Consequently, fertility rates have dropped from above seven in the 1970s to around 2.8 currently.

[141] Reference 136, Figure 13

[142] *Earth in the Balance.* Al Gore (1992) p. 312

[143] http://www.unicef.org/gender/files/Algeria-Gender-Eqaulity-Profile-2011.pdf

Education helps! This phenomenon is also clear from Figure 5-7, which list the time it took to drop the fertility rate from above six to below three. Note that the first four countries took a relatively long time, since this was done well before the ascent of modern contraceptives. Catching up later goes faster! And education again plays a vital role here.

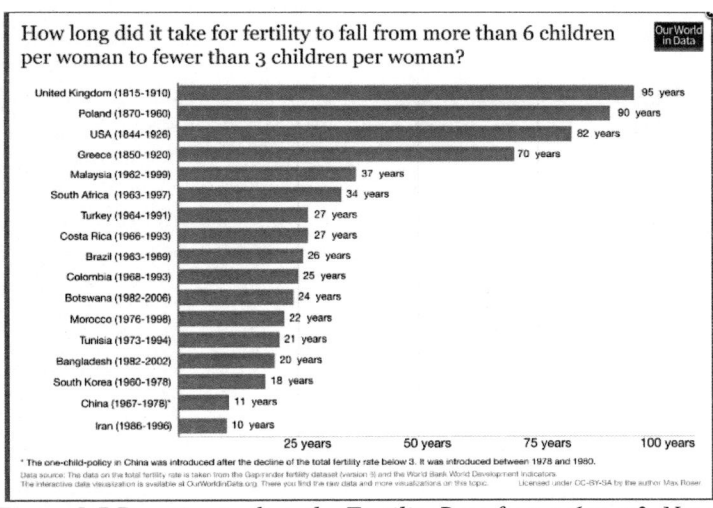

Figure 5-7 Duration to drop the Fertility Rate from >6 to <3. Note that first four countries managed to do this without modern contraceptives, but it took consequently longer.[144]

Unfortunately, the freedom of birth control is still not considered a basic human right. It is not explicitly mentioned in the Universal Declaration of Human Rights and one can only derive this implicitly from other freedom statements. In other UN documents statements on the freedom of birth control are only mentioned as recommendations.[145] The main reason is probably the lobbying of pro-life activists and religious groups, who

---

[144] Max Roser (2016) – '*Fertility*'. Published online at
OurWorldInData.org. Retrieved from: https://ourworldindata.org/fertility/
[145] World Population Plan of Action (WPPA), Bucharest (1974),
International Conference of Population and Development, Cairo (1994)

consider abortion and birth control by means of contraception the same evil. Commitments made at UN conferences more than 20 years ago, do not seem to be implemented as a result. Instead misuse has been reported by government officials (forceful sterilisation or fitting IUD's without choice or information).[146]

And let's face it, the same pro-life lobby is often also a pro-virginity lobby, teaming up with religious pressure groups. Female virginity before marriage in the Muslim world for example is hypocritical, sexist and patriarchal, since Muslim men can do anything they want before marriage. I have met a young, educated Tunisian man, who prided himself on sleeping with many European women, but only wanting to commit himself to a virgin Muslim bride. Desired female virginity requires total absence of contraception and even if contraception is tolerated within marriage, the availability of contraceptive material is considered taboo in many conservative religious Muslim, Catholic, Hindi or Orthodox-Jewish countries and societies.

---

[146] https://rewire.news/article/2012/07/11/looking-human-rights-at-family-planning-summit/

Chapter 6
Migration, War and Human Suffering

Space

As much as we are social animals, we also need some degree of own space. Most of us would desire a room of one's own not just for privacy but also for one's own development. Without being well-off, this is difficult to materialise for larger families. I was one of four siblings and had to share a bedroom with another brother until I left home to study. It was not a big hardship, but life would definitely improve with a private room. Although some people have fond memories sharing a room with one or more siblings, it is relatively rare to prefer this over a room of one's own. Some privacy is like heaven after a day of being social together in play or work or meeting the family. One can read a book, work on a hobby and studying is much easier in a private room.

But it can be worse: some people live in such overcrowded conditions that they all sleep together in the same room or dormitory, sometimes they even do not have a bedroom and the single room is reconstructed every evening and morning. Millions of people live in conditions, where noise or sanitary conditions can irritate people immensely. Conflicts are easily born this way.[147]

However, in more traditional societies in the past and even now, people have lived and slept very close together (e.g. the Inuit's igloo or the Mongolian yurt are classic remaining examples). But these traditional arrangements of sharing all living

---

[147] http://www.nytimes.com/2012/04/15/world/africa/in-nigeria-a-preview-of-an-overcrowded-planet.html

space seem to occur at very low population densities. Living close together is almost an antidote to the vastness of the steppes, tundra or icefields, in which the community is located. Living close together is a form of safety and security against this big frightening outside world. One can have all the privacy one desires in the nature, away from the living quarters and prying eyes.

The sharing of all living space has gradually changed over time, when agricultural food security allowed the human population to increase. More and more people started to live closer together and security and safety gradually improved by taking turns to defend the settlement, later by having city walls and again later by having a dedicated defence force or police. But with increased population density within the walls of a settlement, people started to have more requirements for private living arrangements. However, the combination of poverty and a high fertility rate prevented the large majority of people to live in more private conditions. This only improved as people got richer or got their fertility rate under control. At first, core families compartmentalised from a larger tribal arrangement, followed by separate rooms for children and parents. Almost everybody in the western world now have separate (bed)rooms. It is a stark opposite from traditional living: due to absence of vast open space in cities and towns, people are now glad to retreat to a private room, not to be alone with nature, but to be alone anyway.

In the 1960s some research was carried out on space between humans. According to anthropologist Edward Hall, we are apparently walking around with four spheres around us (see Figure 6-1):[148]

i. The smallest zone, called '*intimate space*', extends outward from our bodies 50 cm in every direction, and only family, pets and one's closest friends may enter. A mere acquaintance hanging out in our intimate space gives us the '*heebie-jeebies*'.

ii. Next in size is the bubble, Hall called '*personal space*', extending from 50 cm to 125 cm away. Friends and acquaintances can comfortably occupy this zone,

[148]http://www.livescience.com/20801-personal-space.html

especially during informal conversations, but strangers are strictly forbidden.

iii. Extending from 1.25 to 3.5 m away from us is '*social space*', in which people feel comfortable conducting routine social interactions with new acquaintances or total strangers.

iv. Beyond there is '*public space*', open to all.

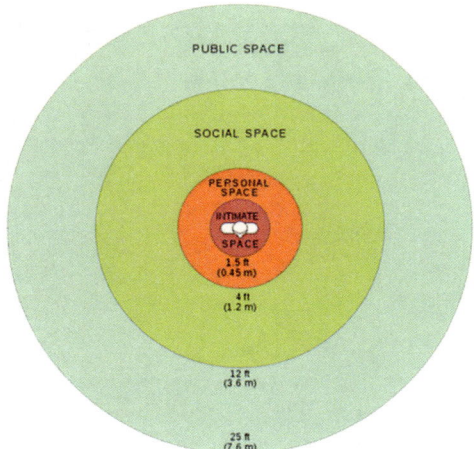

Figure 6-1: Split up of personal space in four spheres according to Edward Hall[148]

In high-density accommodations, people are living and working very close together and there does not seem room for private space. People start to shield themselves off each other in another way by headphones, earphones or staring mindlessly at phone screens. In a world of much reduced space, social interactions in the same space seem to diminish. For the young generation, personal life is now happening more in a virtual world of social media or the Internet. Also at work, space is ever reducing: office cubicles are now intruding in the smallest circles of personal space, with all its irritations and potential conflicts.

It is no wonder that laws and regulations kicked off seriously when people started to live closer together. Without them there would be chaos and only the law of the jungle would prevail. And laws proliferated massively: the British tax code alone is 17000 pages long. A glance at the traffic signs of an average street in Western Europe makes it clear that we regulate our traffic profoundly. It is understandable that people in very rural and sparsely populated parts of a country are wary of all the laws and regulations, created in far-away capitals; for these people a lot less regulation is needed.

But everybody has this deep sensation of limitlessness and awe of vast open space. The exhilaration of speeding a car on deserted roads in the vastness of rural western Spain or the American West, has given me a profound feeling of freedom. Vast open space also has a spiritual sense and beauty and its quietness soothes our souls. I sleep noteworthy better in the countryside than in a noisy city. After all we are descending from a savannah animal, so our yearning for open space and its associated feeling of freedom is understandable.

Borders

With the need for space and an increasing population comes the need for borders. For our Stone Age ancestors, borders were largely physical: a mountain ridge, a big river or a desert provided barriers, which were hard to cross. Gradually within these borders, different cultures (and consequently languages) started to develop, because cultures in isolation mutate too (the idea of a meme).[149] Within these physical borders nationhood was born. The more time a culture had, the more imprinted that culture became in that particular area. A historical cultural border was born.

Not all borders are physical, some borders are manmade. Manmade borders started in the domestic area and were extended to a fertile area with bumper harvests; to a mine, bringing the community great wealth in trade; surrounding an oasis within a desert to provide a community with precious water. Manmade borders were initially meant to protect against theft, but they developed quickly into barriers to keep anybody out so that wealth could accumulate and be passed over to the next generation. Man is greedy. Most billionaires of today have their own security force

---

[149] *The Selfish Gene*. Richard Dawkins (1976)

for protection, live behind fences in a gated community and barely share their wealth with anybody else. Manmade borders are always erected by the wealthy, whilst the have-nots want, but do not get, a borderless world.

Peacefully erasing borders, as the EU has done, seems unique and progressive in historical perspective. The Schengen area even allows free movement of people across national borders. I lived my youth in the southwest of the Netherlands, close to border with Belgium. The changes I have noticed were substantial: first the barrier at the border post, which closed at night, disappeared. Passing the border was thus reduced to nothing more than slowing down and waiting for the nod of the border guard to move on. Hardly any time a passport was asked. Then the border guards disappeared. Nowadays one does not even slow down, and you only know that you are in Belgium by watching the style of the houses.

Some borders are drawn as lines in the sand (e.g. Saudi Arabia, Syria, Jordan) or originate from colonial days (e.g. Sudan, Congo), without any considerations for cultural unity or cohesion. In recent days, relatively little of these borders are allowed to be redrawn and are vehemently defended. These artificial borders only seem to disappear or change by wars and human suffering (e.g. South Sudan, former Yugoslavia) and only very few examples exist of an amicable settlement, such as the split of Czechoslovakia into the Czech Republic and Slovakia. It is time to have another, more grown-up look at national borders in this era of globalisation.

Redrawing borders brings up the worst greed in people: some megalomaniac dictators, monarchs or presidents only seem to be concerned by geopolitical issues; their power only driven by the total area or number of inhabitants of a country, irrespective of their happiness or the costs to forcefully keep large minority groups under control. To give up the historical domination of minority groups in corners of a country, seems to provoke almost traumatic feelings. Nationalism or racism often comes in between when discussing to redraw borders. Figure 6-2 is showing an example of a redrawn map of Europe (I do not necessarily agree;

that the web reference is German[150] comes as no surprise…). I can see loads of people staring at this map, already fuming with anger, so deep is nationalism imbedded in our genes.

Figure 6-2: Alternative map with 'sensible' borders drawn in Europe. The areas with dashed lines are autonomous provinces or de facto self-governed. Various alternatives exist in ref.150!

In our modern world, the globalisation movement wants a world without borders but only for companies to produce or trade their goods cheaply. Free movement of people on a global scale is resisted by western governments, since it would be them to foot the bill of cheap labour by providing healthcare, schooling and financial support. The alternative would be a dramatic drop in living standards, which no one wants. Hence factories are moved abroad, together with some highly educated technical specialists or managers. But when one is rich or brings in unique skills, no one is seen as a threat within the borders. The rich are therefore

[150]http://maps-and-tables.blogspot.co.uk/2015/12/3-maps-of-alternative-europe.html

always welcome in the western world. No questions asked on how one's wealth was acquired: "please buy this house or invest into our country; we want your money!" Or to quote Defoe's Moll Flanders, "*With money in the pocket, one is at home anywhere.*"

And yet there is a worldwide drive to reduce borders, caused by the internet revolution, despite frantic efforts of governments to control access in one country. Virtual internet borders and barriers are used as justifications for dictatorial or religious regimes to give their people only the information which does not undermine their position or religious beliefs (e.g. China, Russia, Saudi Arabia).

History teaches us that cultures, wealth and borders are not forever. Technological progress made physical borders disappear (e.g. boats to cross seas, the use of camels to cross deserts). The Chinese wall and the Iron Curtain in Europe disappeared eventually. It is therefore amazing to see new barriers being erected at the Mexican border of the USA or in the southeast of Europe to stop migration, at least temporarily.

Can we do without borders now? I feel (and many with me)[151] that the world is too unequal and going at too different speeds to allow that now. But gradually getting in that direction is a noble thing and progressive. Since the fall of the Iron Curtain, travel within Europe is already a lot easier than 25 years ago, despite borders being erected at its southern flanks (Fortress Europe). Equality and cultural similarity need to be increased, else removal of borders will only cause mass migration. Unfortunately, eradicating poverty and overcoming cultural differences is painfully slow.

Apart from the gradual removal of borders within the EU, there are already very large countries with a homogenous culture in place (e.g. USA, Canada, Russia, China and to a lesser extent India). Note that the largest ten countries make up 50% of the land surface of the earth. But there is also a fear of a borderless world: a global government could end up monopolising our lives and limiting or stamp out cultural diversity. Blandness already exist in large countries such as the USA or China, where a lot looks

---

[151] https://www.youtube.com/watch?v=yJgEnHbLN-I

already very uniform and the media is either restricted (e.g. in China or Russia) or very skewed towards the right (USA).

Wars

Wars have many causes and overpopulation is one of them. This is particular true if food is becoming scarcer in combination with an ethical conflict, although reasons for wars can be very complex. Malthusian wars are not new: it is well known that the Vikings started their raids in the rest of Europe, because they had become too numerous in Scandinavia. The arrival of agriculture there coincided with a climatic warming around 600 A.D, but agriculture soon reached its limits due to short Scandinavian summers and limited arable lands (only 3% of Norway is suitable for agriculture). Hence the overpopulated Vikings started their raids and their western journeys soon after that. Their raids proved very successful not in least as a result of their ingenious ships, which were both suitable for sea and rivers.[152]

Another classic Malthusian war was the war in Rwanda in 1994 between the Hutus and Tutsis.[153] The war probably had hatred and fear at its basis, fostered by a cynical elite. However, Jared Diamond[154] has noted earlier that both Rwanda and Burundi had large increasing populations[155] and in the past, required food increases were supplied by clearing more forests and draining more marshes. The clearing reached a maximum in the late 1980s, when literally every acre of arable land outside national parks was cultivated. Unfortunately, Rwandan agriculture was not so

---

[152] *Collapse*. Jared Diamond (2005). Penguin edition, Chapter 6

[153] Fred Pearce (Peoplequake (2011), Eden Project Books) disagrees with Jared Diamond on the Malthusian character of this war. But Pearce seems to have a strong negative bias to anything remotely Malthusian. He always finds other reasons as the prime reasons (see also his analysis of the Irish potato famine). I agree that there are other reasons than Malthusian wars or famines, but I have no problem labelling something Malthusian when 80% of the reasons carry a Malthusian character.

[154] *Collapse*. Jared Diamond (2005). Penguin edition, Chapter 10

[155] The population density of Rwanda and Burundi is very high in comparison with other African countries due to the very fertile volcanic soil, abundant rain and their relatively high altitude, which safeguarded the population from malaria or the tsetse fly (see ref 11544).

sophisticated as the agriculture in other densely populated such as the Netherlands or Belgium. The Green Revolution in the 1960s caused much-improved crop yields in the Indian subcontinent, but intensified agriculture in Central Africa lagged behind significantly. The Central African agriculture remained largely traditional without any mechanisation and therefore a lot less efficient. The combination of ever increasing family size with a corresponding reduction in arable plot size for each generation, resulted in hunger and conflict.

And population pressure only has to tilt a delicate climatic imbalance to cause conflict and war. There are theories that the severe drought over the period 2006–2010 in Syria, likely because of global climatic changes, caused local agriculture to collapse: the country could no longer feed itself, which was aggravated by the fact that more than one million Iraqi refugees were added to the already bulging population (Syria had a relatively high fertility rate). A lot of rural Syrians abandoned their homes and flooded Syria's cities without any prospects of work. The Syrian government largely ignored these warnings, which spawned violent protest, ending in civil war.[156]

In the case of initiating wars or conflicts, the so-called youth bulge in demography in the age group 15–24 years is even more important than overpopulation in absolute terms.[157] Jack Goldsmith already noted in 2002 that *'major revolutions—the English Revolution of the 17th century, the French Revolution of the 18th century and most 20th century revolutions in developing countries—have occurred where exceptionally large youth bulges were present'*.[158] It is remarkable that from the 88 countries with a youth bulge in 2006, 60 countries were experiencing social trouble.[159] When the gender ratio is influenced by pre-natal scans and abortions in countries such as India or China, this will

---

[156]www.slate.com/blogs/future_tense/2015/03/02/study_climate_change_he lped_spark_syrian_civil_war.html

[157] A youth bulge is defined as having more than 28% of the population in the 15-24 years' category.

[158] *Population and security: how demographic change can lead to violent conflict.* J. Int. Affairs 56, 3–22. J. Goldstone (2002)

[159]www.ncbi.nlm.nih.gov/pmc/articles/PMC2781832/#RSTB20090151C19

eventually create a surplus of males and might indicate even more troubles ahead. Aggression will occur against internal enemies and external foes.

Sarah Harper in her book *How Population Change will transform our World* has an interesting comparison between youth bulges in the South-East Asia (SEA) and Middle East/North Africa (MENA) regions.[160] She argues that the youth bulge in the SEA region was made to good use in the economies of the Asian Tigers providing what she called a 'demographic dividend' to the countries: the younger generation found work in the booming factories and were responsible for the economic miracle of this region. In contrast the MENA region did not have a demographic dividend, caused by economic prosperity and the MENA youth bulge caused trouble, war and terrorism. What helped the 'demographic dividend' of the SEA region was better leadership, less corruption, better health and education and at the time of the youth bulge, a reducing fertility rate, enabling both men and women to work.

The reverse is also true: conflicts subside once the youth bulge gets older. This happened in Colombia, where the aging of the youth bulge contributed to greater stability after years of guerrilla warfare. An aging population will not go to war and is therefore often a better war deterrent than nuclear weapons. The fertility rate and youth bulge are early warning signals for impending war, which should require serious attention.

Overpopulation alone is no guarantee for war, however. Some countries (e.g. Japan, Bangladesh, The Netherlands and Belgium) have a very high population density but no war has broken out there. They have either a homogeneous ethnic population (e.g. Japan, Bangladesh), no youth bulge (e.g. Japan, Belgium, The Netherlands) or no food shortage. There are many causes for war and they are often interwoven in complexity.

---

[160] *How Population Change Will Transform Our World.* Sarah Harper (2016). Oxford University Press. Chapter 4.

Migrants and Refugees

Homo sapiens started off as a nomadic hunter gatherer. We have maintained that life style for most of our history, bar the last 5000–10000 years. So, migrating is inculcated into our DNA, not because of curiosity, but as a dire necessity. We went where food was present in abundance, away from predators and where the climate was benign. If all those things were available, we stayed put. However, food could become scarce due to climatic changes or when increased numbers could not be fed with the limited food available. That was the moment when we decided to move on. Our curiosity is a derived characteristic from our Stone Age necessities and drove us to discover new sea routes and, more recently, into space.

Population pressure drove Vikings to Iceland and Greenland; it drove impoverished Spanish farmers to Latin America with the conquistadors, and in the 19th and 20th centuries Irish and Italians to the promised lands of North America (as a result of the Irish potato famine or bitter poverty in Italy). More recently, it is population pressure (directly or indirectly because of wars) what is driving the people from sub-Saharan Africa and poorer parts of Asia (e.g. Afghanistan) into Europe.

There are however crucial differences between historical migrations and the latest one: the Vikings, Spanish and Irish/Italians found a largely empty continent and more importantly both Vikings (mastered steel making) and Spanish (owned guns) had added advantages over the native population. The later Irish and Italian exodus was not based on advantages in an already discovered continent, but more based on trying out one's luck in an exponentially growing economy. The current exodus from Africa and parts of Asia is completely different from the previous ones, since the migrants come helpless[161] with little advantages other than their non-skilled labour in an already stagnant, densely populated Europe or in the US, still recovering

---

[161] Fred Pearce in his book *Peoplequake* (2011, Eden Project Books p.202) quoted Oxford's International Migration Institute in a stunning denial of helplessness that most migrants are an aspirational middle class and that few are fleeing conflict. Worldwide 12.4 million newly displaced refugees in 2015 tell otherwise…

from the 2008–2009 economic crisis, where no opportunities seem to exist.

The numbers are also staggering and in no comparison with earlier exoduses. In 2015 and 2016 almost 200,000 Afghan migrants and refugees were registered in the 27 European member states.[162] Fleeing from oppressive violence, from an eternal war with the Taliban and harsh economic conditions, resulting from a very high fertility rate (the highest in Asia) are the main reasons for this massive migration. But even within Europe mass migration is taken place: the number of Albanians[163] and Kosovars amount to 130,000 together in 2015 alone (see Figure 6-3), which is a considerable part of their population. The Kosovar exodus is likely a remnant from the Kosovo-conflict: Serbians were concerned by the Albanian birth rate in Kosovo and consequently feared that the balance of demographic power was rapidly shifting against the Serbians.

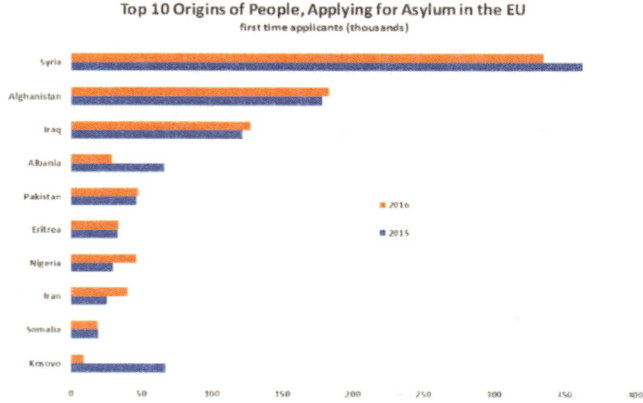

Figure 6-3: Top 10 origins of migrants and refugees in 2015 and 2016, applying for asylum in the EU[164]

---

[162] http://www.voanews.com/content/afghan-emigration-to-europe-seen-as-setback/3124003.html

[163] The Albanian exodus is more related to poverty as a result of long communist rule.

[164]http://ec.europa.eu/eurostat/statistics-explained/index.php/Asylum_statistics

Migration can be too high and cause conflict and can cause a possible cultural implosion: for example, Sweden accepted 160,000 refugees in 2015[165] on a total population of almost 10 million and in Hungary, which has a similar population, the numbers are more than 200,000, see Figure 6-4. Countries which have accepted a lot of asylum seekers are now closing their doors, since they are unable to handle the situation. This is a difficult dilemma: on one hand a country has no right to refuse refugees (unless it has not signed the UNHCR protocol), but numbers can be so overwhelming that a country simply cannot cope. This is even more prevalent in countries which are much poorer, such as countries, neighbouring war zones. However, in those neighbouring countries integration problems may be smaller, since smaller cultural differences exist.

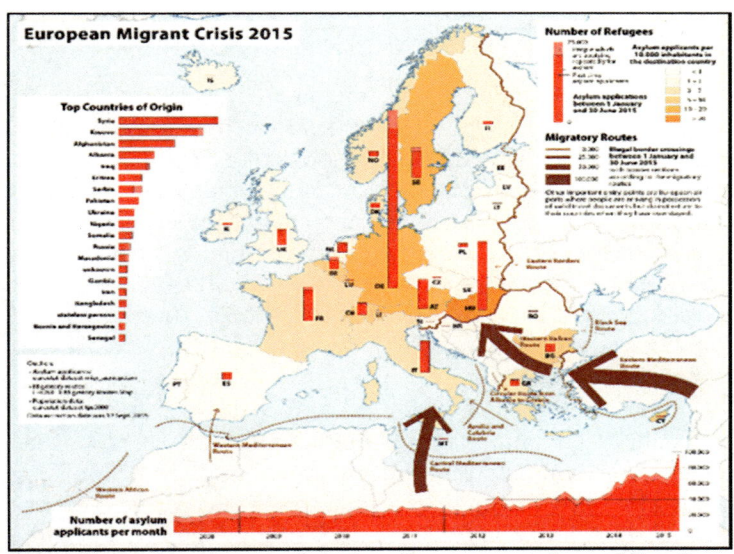

Figure 6-4: Migration numbers into Europe up to the middle of 2015[166]

---

[165] http://dailysignal.com/2015/12/31/sweden-accepted-more-refugees-per-capita-than-any-other-eu-country-now-its-tightening-borders/
[166]Map from Wikipedia, https://en.wikipedia.org /wiki/European_migrant_crisis, Author Maximilian Dörrbecker

Can we stop migration? That is a difficult question. It depends on numbers, the desperation of the migrants and the willingness and kindness of the population of the receiving country. History has taught us that eventually all walls will fall: the Iron Curtain only lasted 35 years. Temporarily this may seem a useful solution, but on the longer term it is probably not. It is hard to stop desperate people: people keep on trying numerous times, by risking their lives. The BBC had an excellent series of programmes,[167] called Exodus, shown in July 2016. They highlighted the many attempts people made until they succeeded entering Europe (or died). It seems an unstoppable flux of people and people in the West can often not comprehend the reasons why people would leave their country. Rather than staring at pictures on television or the Internet, why are people in the West not trying to have some personal experience of the situation in poor and overpopulated countries and thus have a better understanding the reasons behind migration?

Rather than building walls, migration is better stopped by tackling the problems at their roots. Try to resolve wars and try to gradually change the patriarchal, traditional, religious or corrupt cultures to prevent poverty and population explosions, which lie at the basis of modern migration. Another deterrence, used by the Danish government, is to address potential migrants with a letter in local newspapers in areas. In Figure 6-5 the English version of such a letter in a Lebanese newspaper is shown. An article dated 6 months later[168] suggested that the policy of deterrence has worked to some extent.

Economic migration is claimed to be beneficial for both the emigrating as the immigrating country. Fred Pearce mentions the example of Filipino nurses, without whom hospitals and nursing homes in dozens of countries would fail.[169] Economic migrants often send a lot of money home, boosting the GDP of the emigrating country. Unfortunately, this does not always lift these countries out of poverty and can end up in a vicious circle, when

[167] http://www.bbc.co.uk/programmes/b07ky6ft
[168] https://www.hrw.org/news/2016/03/03/dispatches-denmarks-deterrence-tactics-refugees
[169] *Peoplequake*. Fred Pearce (2011) Eden Project Books p.204

remittances are used to educate other family members, who are migrating in turn, because their qualifications earn more money abroad. At worst the remittances of economic migrants are used to perpetuate patriarchal family structures (e.g. dowries).

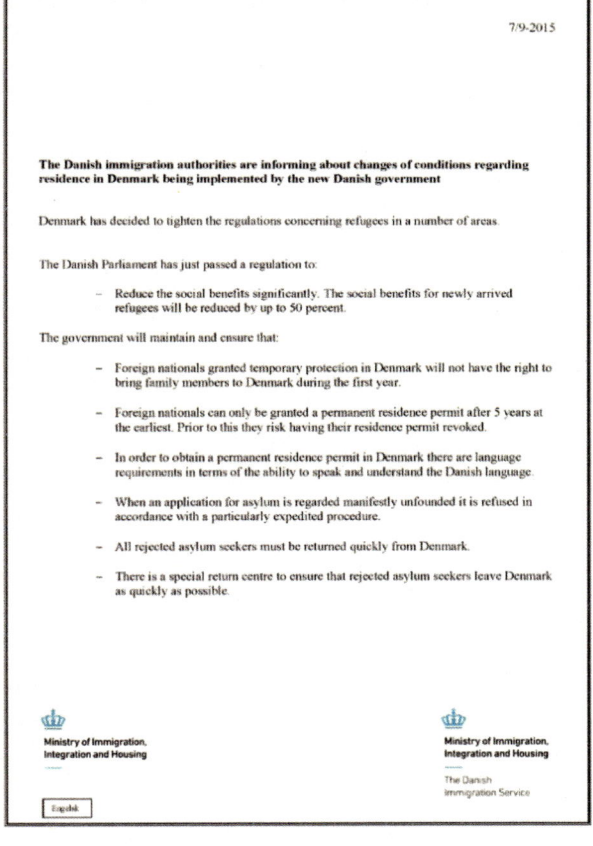

Figure 6-5: Letter by the Danish government appearing in Lebanese newspapers in September 2015[170]

---

[170] http://www.thelocal.dk/20150907/denmarks-anti-refugee-ads-published-in-foreign-papers

103

Human Suffering

Having too many people around has a tremendous effect on people's lives. The first thing coming to mind, is hunger and unemployment resulting from overpopulation. The lives of many people are thus filled in misery, due to undernourishment, poverty, violence, early illness or death. Overpopulation causes a lack of education and creates suppression of wages, resulting in poverty. It traps people in lousy jobs in sweatshops or toiling hard on land or factories. It promotes exploitation and abuse by corrupt businessmen or richer citizens: payday loan companies, sexual abuse, child labour or modern slavery are just a couple of depressing examples.

The absence of employment and consequent poverty in rural areas has driven millions of people to towns and cities. The worldwide urbanisation has already surpassed 50% of the world population. But fast urbanisation causes major problems: due to overcrowding an increasing number of people live in slums (see Figure 6-6). The total amount of slum dwellers in the world is already 1 billion and the number is expected to rise: another 500 million are expected by 2020.[171] Slums come with a lot of misery, ill health and early death due to lack of sanitation[172] and poor leaky buildings. Consequent violence comes as no surprise.

It is with remarkable denial of the misery in the slums that Fred Pearce describes slums as '*places of hope, enterprise and innovation*' and that for '*every gun-toting gangster or terrorist there are 100 romantic would-be slum-dog millionaires*'.[173] These are typical thoughts for a casino capitalist, who extrapolates from an upbeat mainstream movie and waves the real misery away in a couple of apologetic sentences. Unfortunately, the upbeat story in *Slum-dog Millionaire* is just as likely as the misery in the movie *City of Gods*.[174] The fact that Pearce visited some slums (and

---

[171] http://www.citiesalliance.org/node/ 2195

[172] There is one toilet for every 500 people in the slums of Nairobi, Kenya based on ref. 170

[173] *Peoplequake*. Fred Pearce (2011) Eden Project Books p.267

[174] *Slumdog Millionaire* directed by Danny Boyle (2008). *City of Gods* directed by Fernando Meirelles (2002)

probably cherry picked some locations and interviewees), does not make him an authority on the subject.

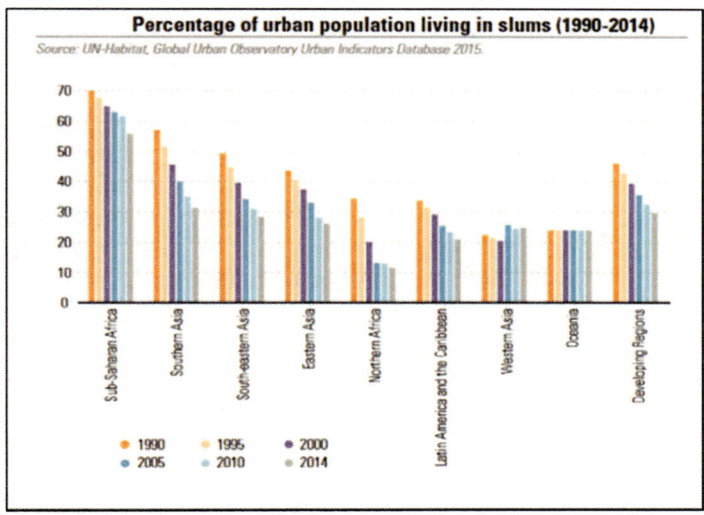

Figure 6-6: Proportions of urban population in the developing world living in slums.[175] Percentage trends are decreasing but absolute numbers are not.

There is also suffering in the overpopulated western world, but in a different way and not at the same scale as in the developing world: we spent sometimes hours in daily traffic jams to commute to work but rarely think what a wasteful time of our life that is. Noise, due to traffic and overcrowded estates, is so disturbing, that it is affecting our sleep and health. Big cities are so full or have a dwindling amount of affordable housing that homelessness is on the rise.

It is often this suffering that drives people away from centres of war or poverty. Unfortunately, their migration is not without suffering either. First, there is an army of profit seekers involved to rob refugees and migrants from their last savings. Often loans are taken out to place a healthy young family member in Europe

---

[175] http://wcr.unhabitat.org/main-report/ Figure 3.1

or US, which is grudgingly spent on people smugglers or other profiteers. The traffickers in Turkey and Libya are notorious to cash in on other people's misery. The Exodus programme[1677] highlighted this heart-breaking profiteering very clearly: Turkish smugglers asked €2000 for a dangerous dingy crossing to Greece, whilst the ferry from Izmir to one of the Greek islands only cost €20; similarly, Libyan traffickers took a West African refugee hostage, demanding even more from his family back home. Smugglers alone made at least $5 billion in 2015[176] and weapon exports from Eastern Europe fuelling wars in Iraq and Syria amounted to more than €1.2 billion over a three-year period preceding 2015.[177] War and misery of others seem to be very beneficial to some despicable vulture-like predators. Their illegally acquired money should be the subject of criminal prosecution, but this is admittedly not the priority for a failed state such as Libya or a corrupt country such as Turkey, where migrant flows are used as political means to get favours from the European Union.

The misery does not stop on the shores of the Mediterranean: 3800 migrants died in 2015 attempting to cross in unsafe boats. Others die 'en route' stuck in or under trucks, trying to cross via ferries, or on railway carriages. Once on location their misery may continue: discrimination, sexual or physical abuse, slavery or at best working illegally at wages, much less than the legal minimum without any benefits. But these horrible statistics do not seem to work as a deterrent, which is something we need to learn to accept.

---

[176]http://www.nytimes.com/2016/05/18/world/europe/migrants-refugees-smugglers.html
[177]https://www.theguardian.com/world/2016/jul/27/weapons-flowing-eastern-europe-middle-east-revealed-arms-trade-syria

Chapter 7
Too Many Siblings

Individual Time and Equal Opportunities

Most modern cultures in the world do not punish children for their parents' background or behaviour and consider that a child is to some extent a blank slate. Although the nature-nurture debate suggests that some of our traits are hereditary, most of us accept that children should be treated equally and have equal opportunities. But taking poverty out of the equation, has every child equal opportunities? Does family size influence equal opportunities, when comparing children from families of different sizes?

Childhood is a learning stage and preparation for adulthood and functions best in a carefree environment. Picking up new things goes so much easier by play and dedicated interaction, when there is no stress around. Play and learning are crucial for a child's development to become successful and well balanced as an adult. Anxieties and stress during childhood can cause mental health problems, delinquency or violent behaviour at a later age.

A lot is written and researched about the amount of time parents should spend with their children. Recently we are beginning to realise that it is equally important to spend time with each child individually and plenty of articles are written on this subject, also offering potential solutions. However, surprisingly little research is carried out on how much time parents should spend with each individual child. Spending time with each child individually will enhance the parent-child bond and reduce attention seeking behaviour. This will build self-confidence and worth in shyer children and communicates that you recognise their individual needs and values.[178] The focus in the many articles, mainly written by mothers, seem to emphasise tactics in big families: for example, to declare a special night each month (e.g. their birth date) to spend 20–30 minutes individually with the child,[179] as if 20–30 minutes' individual time per month is enough… Strategic discussions on spending more time per child or how to avoid spending so little individual time (e.g. by having a smaller family) are notoriously absent.

In absence of research on individual time spent with children within a family, it is maybe wise to turn to schools and nurseries. The amount of time a childminder is supposed to give to each child individually is not known or fixed, but the number of children per carer in childcare is bound by a maximum by law in many European countries.[180] Implicitly this means governments and law-making institutions value a certain minimum amount of time spent on a child individually and also value that a child carer can only handle a maximum number of children. Almost everybody believes that smaller classes are more beneficial to a child (see evidence, albeit not that strong, in Figure 7-1) and therefore there is a strong drive, acknowledging financial considerations, to push for an upper limit in class size in particular for the younger years. However, when it comes to family size, hardly any critiques are heard, since family size is considered almost anywhere as a personal choice.

But to stay with the analogy of the school class: size does not govern everything. It is also the quality and mental prowess of the teacher (or parent) which determines a successful child development. All things being equal however, size does matter.

---

[178]http://amotherfarfromhome.com/the-importance-of-spending-time-with-your-children-individually/

[179] http://www.yourmodernfamily.com/spending-one-on-one-time-with-your-kids/

[180]https://www.gov.uk/government/uploads/system/uploads/attachment_data/file/219660/More_20Great_20Childcare_20v2.pdf

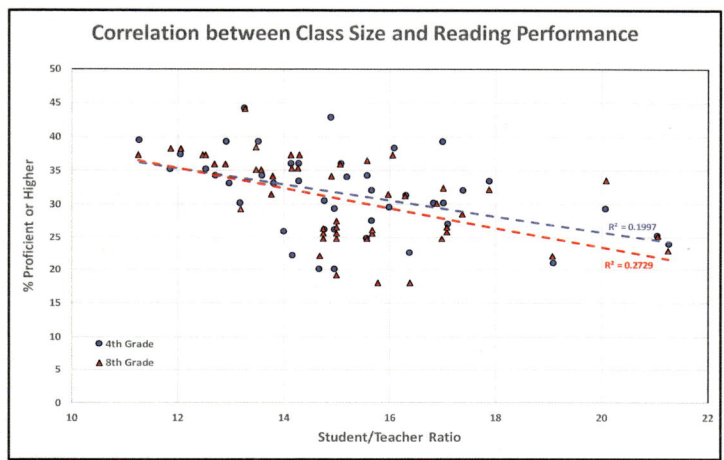

Figure 7-1: US evidence of better pupil performance for small classes[181]

A better educational achievement is strongly correlated with smaller family size, although in some countries which score high on the collectivism scale (help from family members or other villagers), the correlation is less clear or can even go the other way around.[182] In less traditional societies, where children can only rely on core family members, a large family influences schooling results. Due to globalisation and migration to cities, the more traditional societies, relying on an extended family or even the village, are in decline. In fact, one of the reasons of a reducing fertility rate of urban populations is likely a direct result of the absence of child care or educational support by an extended family.

Due to their ignorance and/or perpetuating misery (*"we did not get attention from our parents either…"*), some poor parents do not believe giving their children individualised attention because in their eyes that is equivalent to babying and spoiling

[181] Data from https://www.quora.com/Does-class-size-affect-educational-outcomes

[182]http://paa2015.princeton.edu/uploads/151825

them. This is a shameful argument used by often bitter parents, who deserve our pity. The same rationale is also used to justify the continuation of FGM. Together we should try to break these vicious circles in poor families.

Sibling Cooperation and Rivalry

Sibling rivalry has its roots in the amount of attention obtained from parents. The more time is spent with a child to read a book at bedtime, to talk about school over tea or to learn how to fix a bicycle tyre, the more it will enhance the parent-child relationship which is healthy for a child's development. It is a no-brainer that with more siblings around, parental attention needs to be shared. To share attention is not necessarily a bad thing, but with large families and/or working parents, attention per child can drop dangerously low. However, when there is strong competition for parental attention, often closer sibling bonds develop, because they feel part of a team.[183] Milevsky in ref. 183 further quotes that *'Studies actually do show that children from larger families are more likely to be altruistic, cooperative, and interdependent than children from smaller families',* but he fails to reference those studies. That is likely to be true, but it highlights only the good outcomes of frequent social interaction. Equally true is that frequent social interaction can be a breeding ground for developing bullies, crooks or psychopaths. Milevsky also quotes that *'siblings in larger families have more options of siblings to interact with, creating sibling subgroups, which may contribute to closer sibling relationships'.* But there are also negative sides to closer sibling relationships since sibling subgroups can easily lead to insular or tribal behaviour, which is not good for the cohesion of the family, nor for the children's development. All that can be said from these studies and observations is that large families have more opportunity for social interaction. To highlight only the positive outcomes seems incomplete.

It is difficult to judge family size objectively, since so many other factors play a role. The mental ability, education and

[183]https://www.psychologytoday.com/blog/band-brothers-and-sisters/201207/fighting-piece-mom-family-size-and-sibling-relationships

financial strength of the parents all are important factors. There are always exceptions but too often large family size correlates strongly positive with poverty, poorly educated parents or with fractured families (single mothers or with multiple fathers). In that context, the above mentioned potential positive characteristics get masked by other more negative factors.

Sibling rivalry or aggression is not new, even the Bible tells us the story of Cain and Abel and what happened to them. A study[184] concluded that sibling aggression was found to be widespread, with 46% of all participants being victimised and 36% perpetrating aggression. The study also mentioned that a large family size, male siblings, and financial difficulties were associated with greater rates of sibling aggression. Sibling aggression can cause bullying and mental aberrations in later life. Children from large families tend to have more criminal behaviour.[185]

In smaller families, there is likely to be less sibling rivalry and a greater opportunity to develop an independent and rounded personality. Children with no or few siblings likely benefit from more contacts with children from other families and be involved in adult activities rather than being cocooned in an insular set of siblings. They can be more self-sufficient, mature and well-behaved. Research has also shown that single children do just as well in later life as other children.[186,187]

Debunking the myth of the only child as spoilt, overprotected, selfish or lonely has not proven to be easy and stereotypes persist. The myth originated from American psychologist Granville Stanley Hall[188] in his book *Of Peculiar and Exceptional Children (1896)*, in which he described a series of only-child oddballs as permanent misfits. He as much claimed that '*being an only child is a disease in itself*'. Of course, people invest more in a single

[184] http://www.ncbi.nlm.nih.gov/pubmed/25187483

[185] https://www.washingtonpost.com/news/wonk/wp/2016/01/01/small-families-are-better-for-kids-according-to-new-research/?wpisrc=nl_draw

[186] https://www.populationmatters.org/take-action/consume-less/small-family/

[187] http://content.time.com/time/magazine/article/0,9171,2002530-2,00.html

[188] https://en.wikipedia.org/wiki/G._Stanley_Hall

child than when they have more than one child and consequently they are probably more protective too. But that single children are more selfish or lonely, is largely disproved.

Due to birth order phenomena, inequality and favouritism is more widespread in large families.[189] If a person truly states that he/she loves being from a large family, chances are that they are the youngest in their families. The youngest child in a large family has the least responsibilities, often has a more carefree childhood than their elder siblings who were usually saddled with household and caretaking responsibilities from a very young age. They can get away with things for which their elder siblings would be severely punished. Middle children may feel more left out, due to lack of responsibilities, mainly given to the eldest sibling(s) but also lacking the carefree existence of the youngest child. They either fade into the background, become shy and withdrawn or seek attention by becoming loud or aggressive.

Supporting Mum and Dad: Child Labour and Child Carers

Large families are often poor families. They can be cause and effect: poverty creates large families to supply cheap labour in agricultural and backward communities. Large families may create poverty because of the many mouths to feed. When financial difficulties prevail, the eldest children are often send out to support the parents financially and implicitly to feed the many younger siblings. Before she was married, my own mother, who was the eldest in her family, had to give all her earnings as a secretary to my grandparents, since they were unable to make ends meet for her other five siblings.

There are miserable stories of eldest children, wasting their best child years in support of their siblings. Many people even resented their parents by having more children than they could properly care for. An article quotes that many eldest children in large and very large families *'actually hate their parents for*

---

[189]http://hubpages.com/family/The-Inequality-Of-The-Large-Family-System

placing such an onus on them'.[190] There is a heart-breaking story in the Exodus programmes[191] about a Gambian teenager, forced to risk his life to reach Europe (desert crossing, Libyan prison) to find work in support of his single mother and younger siblings.

According to UNICEF[192] an estimated 150 million children worldwide are involved in child labour. A child is considered to be involved in child labour under the following UNICEF conditions:

- children 5–11 years old who carry out at least one hour per week of economic activity or at least 28 hours per week of household chores
- children 12–14 years old who carry out at least 14 hours per week of economic activity or at least 28 hours per week of household chores

There is a strong correlation between child labour and fertility rate (or family size or poverty), as Figure 7-2 indicates. Some off-trend countries have been highlighted by name. Post-war data from Iraq and East Timor do seem not reliable at first glance. As with the high fertility data, the highest number of children involved in child labour are from Sub-Saharan Africa.

Labouring children can turn into child carers, when one of the parents drops out due to illness, death or divorce. This is not an exclusive large family phenomenon, but it is more prevalent in large families, due to the generally bigger age difference between the youngest and eldest child. It is often the eldest child stepping in: when the mother drops out, the eldest daughter is forced to step in caring for her siblings at home; when the father drops out, the eldest son is forced to make a living and support the rest of the family. The burden on such young overworked and underappreciated children is often too much and stress is a common result on these sibling mums and dads. The argument that

[190] Ibid.

[191] http://www.bbc.co.uk/programmes/b07ky6ft

[192] http://data.unicef.org/child-protection/child-labour.html Data from May 2016.

early responsibility is good for them, is an unfair evasion of parental responsibility.

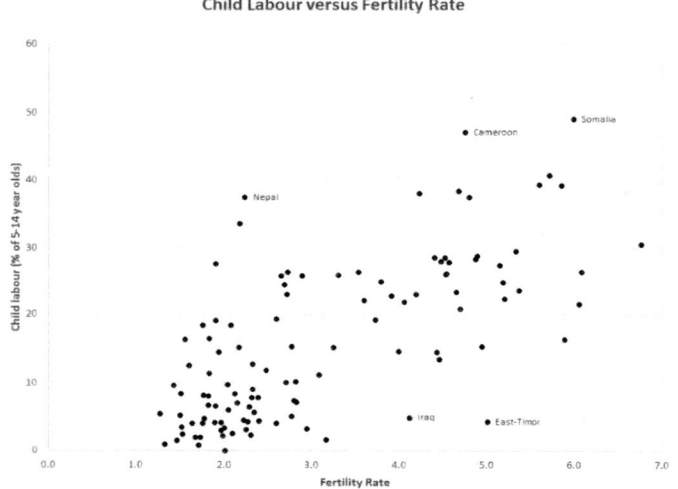

Figure 7-2 Child labour is more prevalent in larger families (data by country) [192,193]

On the receiving end, sibling mums and dads have less parental experience than adults, resulting in tensions for the younger children, because they do not get the care they need. It can result in dangerous situations (e.g. unsafe handling of babies, unsafe use of gas for cooking) and may lead that sibling parents are fed up with caring, since they lack the resilience of an adult (e.g. sleep deprivation). Younger children being cared for by a sibling parent, receive therefore a lot less quality care than from adult parents. Psychological problems at later age often originate from the toiling days as a sibling mum or dad.

In England and Wales, it is estimated that there are 250,000 child carers (around 2.5% of the age group 5–19 years) and 23,000

[193]Fertility data from CIA Fact book data
https://en.wikipedia.org/wiki/List_of_sovereign_states_and_dependent_terri
tories_by_fertility_rate

are younger than 9 years,[194] see Figure 7-3. This probably should be seen as the tip of the iceberg. In the developing world, these numbers are likely to be much higher, due to stronger likelihood of disease (e.g. AIDS), early death and larger families, which require more support if one of the parents drops out.

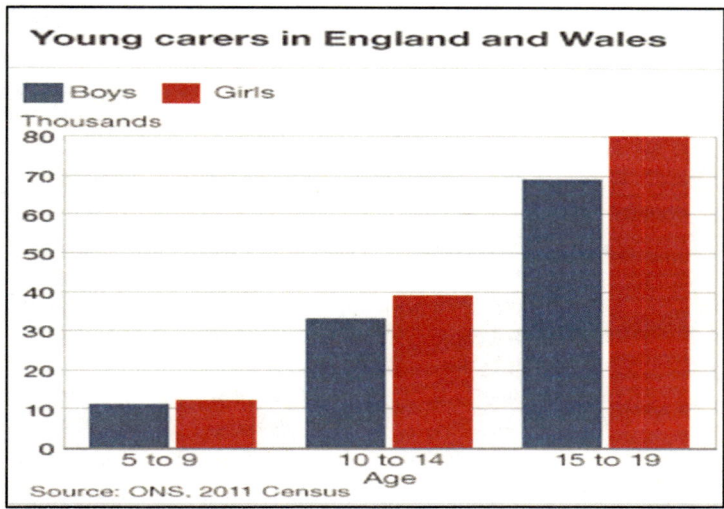

Figure 7-3: A quarter of a million child carers existed in England and Wales in 2011

Fractured Families

To manage a large family is stressful. It is quite easy to lean back and let the children sort out themselves out on their own. Since the majority of large families are poor families, illness or premature death are more likely. And then there are the coward husbands, who created a large family in the first place and then escape this misery, leaving a large family to fend for itself. To handle a large family with only one parent is extremely hard and makes the remaining parent constantly work in overdrive. Children from a divorced family need to cope already a lot with their new situation and the divorced parents are often so

---

[194] http://www.bbc.co.uk/news/education-22529237

destabilised and embroiled in their own new situation, that it is difficult to give enough support to the individual child, helping to adapt. This is only aggravated when a divorced parent needs to take care of a large number of children. It is therefore logical to expect that neglect is more prevalent when there are many children. Surprisingly little research is carried out on the correlation between large and fractured families.

And a variety on the theme of fractured families is when another man arrives in the deserted family and creates another offspring with the mother (domino-dads).[195] This can go well and there are ample examples which show that the situation moves for the better. After all, second families seem better than fractured families. Unfortunately, there is also a lot of evidence that favouritism, sexual and physical abuse are more prevalent in families with children of multiple fathers. These blurred intra-family boundaries are also breeding ground for sibling incest[196] in particular in large families where lack of parental supervision is more prevalent.

Large families with one parent or a substitute parent have limited parental control and are easy prey for all kinds of abuses. The Turkish movie *Mustang* (Deniz Ergüven, 2015) shows what can happen when both mum and dad are gone and five young girls are raised by their grandmother, who is incapable to control them; sexual abuse happened when an uncle sneaked in the bedroom of one of the girls. I am sure that abuse would occur less frequently when the grandmother would only care for one or two children.

The street will take care of them

Fractured families can be so overwhelmed by poverty traps, sexual or physical abuse that a child decides to escape. The saying 'streetwise' is both a compliment (having a fighting spirit and knowing one's way around) as it has a negative connotation, with undertones of theft, violence or prostitution. Homeless children

---

[195] http://healthland.time.com/2011/04/01/the-prevalence-of-the-domino-dad-family/

[196] *http://www.socialworktoday.com/archive/111312p18.shtml*

are very vulnerable and are much more prone to criminal behaviour, abuse by thugs or forced into child slavery (sex or work).

There are cultural differences in the world with respect to child raising. In the developed world, where core families are the norm, we all feel responsible for our own children. However, this is not necessary the case in the developing world, such as Africa or India. Indigenous fathers in India claim that *'a child is the responsibility of the community'*.[197] The 'State of the World's Fathers' report (ref. 197) is quite mild and sees the community more as an addition to parental care. However more extreme opinions exist, particularly in poorer areas.

A large family size may be one of the reasons why children leave home prematurely. An Indian study[198] quotes that 75% of street children originate from a family size larger than four. Correlating street children with family size is difficult, since the definition of street or homeless children is rather blurred. Street children may refer to children making a living on the streets, but still return to their parents in the evening. Homeless children may refer to children living with their homeless parents, due to poverty, war or migration. Most estimates for street children are ranges: for example, it is estimated that there are between 20 and 50 million street children in Latin America. The large range suggests how difficult it is to have reliable estimates.[199]

In India, there are between 18 and 44 million[199] street children or roughly between 5% and 13% of the population in the cohort between 5 and 18 years. On the African continent, the estimate of street children amounts to 32 million, of which 11 million are orphans[199]. This equates to 15% of the population of African children between 5 and 18 years. There is an implicit link with large families, when inspecting the high fertility rates (India above 3 in 2000 and Africa well above 5 in 2000).

---

[197]http://sowf.s3.amazonaws.com/wp-content/uploads/2015/06/08181421/State-of-the-Worlds-Fathers_23June2015.pdf Page 67.
[198] Street Children and the Asphalt Life, P.C. Shukla (2005) p. 60
[199]http://www.youthxchange.net/main/b236_homeless-h.asp

Disadvantaged children on the street are easy prey for abusers, for the drugs trade (70% of Latin America's street children are estimated to be addicted to glue[199]) or for extremist purposes. The shy neglected children of a large family or children dumped on the street could be swept up, brainwashed and radicalised by Islamic extremists, since their education is generally poor. They seek glory as a suicide bomber or fighter in the Middle East, since anything is better than their current miserable existence.

It is time to reconsider why we are putting children in the world. Too often it is just a result of sexual intercourse without any considerations for the circumstances of the future child. Too often this has been promoted by the established classes to provide cheap labour or to end up as cannon-fodder. Their religious cronies are feeding uneducated people with guilt or reminding them of outdated cultural prejudices. Before raising an unlimited number of children, the potential misery of children, having to care for parents or fending for themselves on the streets, should be seriously considered.

A lot of prospective parents also underestimate the costs to raise a child. Recently a lot of articles have appeared both in the developed world[200,201] and the developing world,[202] improving the awareness of these costs. Of course, numbers can be debated, but, without having to compromise a child's future, the larger the family size the more money is needed. Most people have finite budgets, hence larger families normally have to compromise. So, let us look at the perspective of parents as well.

[200]https://www.theguardian.com/lifeandstyle/2016/feb/16/cost-of-raising-children-in-uk-higher-than-ever
[201]http://www.thesimpledollar.com/can-you-afford-to-have-kids-a-pre-baby-financial-checklist/
[202]http://economictimes.indiatimes.com/which-investment-option-is-the-best-for-your-childs-future/estimate-the-cost-of-raising-your-child/slideshow/8007024.cms

Chapter 8
Parenting and Nothing Else?

Fulfilling Lives

What separates us from the animal kingdom is our choice to make life decisions. At the dawn of humanity, we were probably more animal-like and procreation was therefore the one and only goal in life. Since we are social animals as well, we care for the old, weak and ill. Having children was therefore seen as a guarantee for old age to ensure free care and food. Since child mortality was high, fertility was high too, so that at least a couple of children survived to guarantee a stress-free old age.

This animal behaviour gradually started to wane once we got an appetite for other things in life, such as interests in a hobby, art or science. Child rearing was until very recently the domain of women: it was considered normal for men to hunt, then labour on the fields, in factories or mines and leave the task of raising children almost exclusively to women. Due to the sheer number of children, child rearing was a career for life for most of the women, apart from the very elite, who could count on child minders or had fewer children, because more survived.

Although having children gives meaning to our life, it is not a great fulfilment in life just to raise children. A 2007 study in the US indicated that only 41% of married couples are saying that children are very important for a successful marriage, down from 65% in 1990.[203] As a young woman, my grandmother was a schoolteacher in the 1920s. After marriage, she abruptly stopped

---

[203]http://www.pewsocialtrends.org/2007/07/01/as-marriage-and-parenthood-drift-apart-public-is-concerned-about-social-impact/

her career and raised six children, who needed all her attention. After having worked as a secretary, the same happened to my mother: raising four children at the same time as running the shop of my paternal grandparents was a fulltime job. Her job became 'house wife', with no further development or enrichment of her life.

What happened in the past in the developed world, is still happening in strongly religious countries, such as in Spain until 1980 (although it has caught up a lot since the years immediately following Franco's death) and Saudi Arabia, where women are allowed to study and work, until they marry and have children (see also Figure 8-1). In Africa, women are having jobs, but due to dire economic reasons and in spite of having a larger family size. The jobs they have are not fulfilling any development either: both African women and men lead a subsistence life.

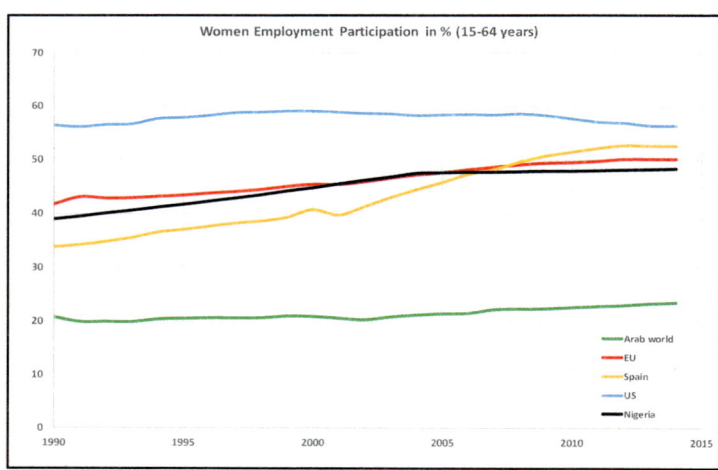

Figure 8-1: Women employment participation rate between 1990 and 2014 in selected countries. Note the low numbers for the Arab World and the rising numbers in Spain after the Catholic Church started to lose its grip on the country[204]

[204] Data from http://data.worldbank.org/indicator /SL.TLF.CACT.FE.ZS

Despite having fewer children than in the past, the time to parent in the western world has not reduced. In fact, parents (in particular men) in the western world seem to spend a lot more time and money per child in comparison with the past. This has a lot of positive benefits for the children, such as more educational assistance, more general care and love, safety and security or the ability to go on vacation, to develop in sports, just to name a few. Due to social pressures (neighbours, media) parental care can be exaggerated and some parents in the western world are more like slaves for being 24 hours per day and 7 days a week available to their children. These children take priority over everything and some parents go as far as letting their children decide where to go on holiday. This parenting style is bound to fail, with parents exhausted during school holidays[205] or some others relaxing in the office ('*it feels like a holiday after being at home*').[206]

In the western world contraceptives became widespread available during the 1960s and at the same time religious or cultural pressures reduced. The number of children gradually transformed from a lottery outcome after each sexual intercourse, to a choice for everyone. That choice resulted in a big reduction of children per couple.

Research has been carried out to correlate parental happiness with the number of children. In his analysis of a survey of 35,000 Danish twins, Hans-Peter Kohler found that women with one child said they were more satisfied with their lives than women with none or more than one[206]. It is realised that Denmark is considered the happiest country in the world, but one can question whether happiness is culturally defined and hence Danish happiness may not be universal. However, there are more signals that fewer or no children are increasingly desired:

1. The increase of urbanisation and a consequent increase of core families required an adaption of family size over time. Absence of an extended family necessitated paid childcare, which is costly however. In urban areas, space

[205]https://www.theguardian.com/commentisfree/2016/jul/22/working-parents-dread-summer-holidays-pokemon-go-children
[206]http://www.slate.com/articles/double_x/doublex/2013/06/why_one_child_is_enough_for_me_all_of_the_joy_less_of_the_crap.html

is limited and housing is therefore smaller or more expensive than in the countryside. Although not a desire per se, the ongoing movement from rural areas to cities[207] is therefore an important driver to limit family size.

2. After the abolishment of the one child rule in China, a large proportion of the couples did not go for more children. Although this is mainly governed by economic reasons (salary, childcare, housing), the parental career and success for the child were also important considerations. When parents of only children were asked how much children they wanted without any economic restrictions, their initial answer was two[208] but no more.

3. In countries where people have the freest choice and where the lowest gender inequality occurs, such as Scandinavia, the Benelux and France, child care is heavily subsidised. Fertility rates in those countries are hovering around 2.0 (see figure 2-9) and not more.

And of course there are other views of what needs to come first, procreation or fulfilment. About 20 years ago, one of my brothers commented on the choice of my youngest brother of not having children as selfish: in other words, the fulfilment of one's life should be subordinate to the goal of procreation.[209] On a much larger scale operates the powerful right-wing pro-life movement in the US, with heavy religious indoctrination. It even suggested that the UN is '*brainwashing* Kenyan women into wanting fewer children',[210] without realising that they are brainwashed themselves. Telling the truth about sustainability in African countries is seen by these zealots as '*undisguised eugenics*'.

---

[207]http://www.un.org/en/development/desa/news/population/world-urbanization-prospects-2014.html

[208]https://www.washingtonpost.com/opinions/chinese-parents-can-now-have-more-than-one-child-why-many-say-they-wont/2014/01/10/2c9811de-73c5-11e3-8def-a33011492df2_story.html?utm_term=.32b4f84e790c

[209] Luckily, he abandoned his views and my youngest brother got a child at late age.

[210]http://www.thenewamerican.com/world-news/africa/item/17291-un-unveils-plot-to-reduce-african-population

Is Everybody Fit to Parent?

Apart from strongly religious or patriarchal regions, people have a choice in the number of children they want. But is everybody fit or ready to parent? Several reasons should be considered when discussing parental fitness: age, mental health, physical health and environmental circumstances. In the Netherlands and Denmark, certified child workers, must train for three years after the age of 18,[211] but for parents, age limits to start a family are not compulsory. Adoptive or foster parents are required to be older than 21 years of age, financially stable and responsible mature adults.[212] In fact, in many countries people are allowed to marry and procreate at a much lower age whilst training prospective parents in child raising is only ridiculed in the majority of countries.

In several African countries, the first-born child has on average a teenage mother and quite a lot of countries have mothers, who have their first born, when less than 25 years old (see Figure 8-2). Brain development reaches maturity in the period between 20 and 25 years and valid questions are raised whether 25 years is not a better cut-off point for adulthood.[213] Moreover, people in the western world often are studying well into their twenties, which is difficult to combine with raising a child. The period between 20 and 25 years should therefore be considered as a grey area regarding parental fitness.

The United Nations has gathered statistics on the age of parents by country over the period 2003–2012.[214] Although incomplete (unfortunately, very few African countries are represented due to lack of data), it highlights a couple of stark differences in the world. Figure 8-3 shows the three critical age categories for motherhood (<15 years, 15–19 years and 20–24

---

[211]https://www.gov.uk/government/uploads/system/uploads/attachment_dat a/file/219660/More_20Great_20Childcare_20v2.pdf

[212]http://www.first4adoption.org.uk/who-can-adopt-a-child/

[213] http://www.bbc.co.uk/news/magazine-24173194

[214] UN Demographic yearbook 2012, Table 10 and 11. Data are not always from the same years. http://unstats.un.org/unsd/demographic/products/dyb/ dyb2012.htm

years). The data have been sorted from the highest occurrence of percentage teenage mothers downwards.

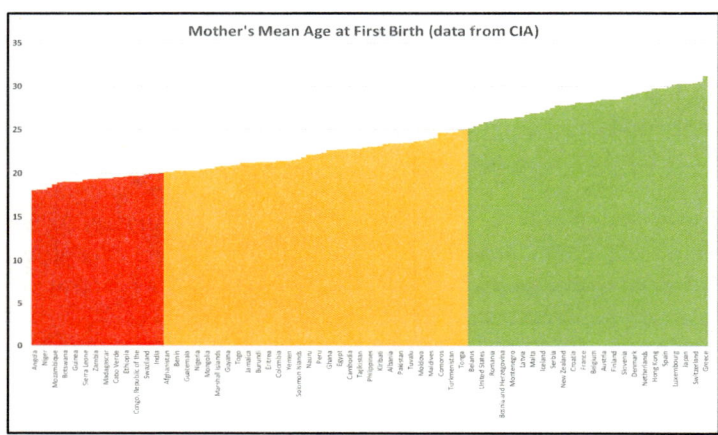

Figure 8-2: Mother's Mean Age at first Birth. Red < 20 years, orange between 20 and 25 years, green >25 years.[215] Not all countries in the world are represented and data are not always gathered in the same year (period 2007–2013).

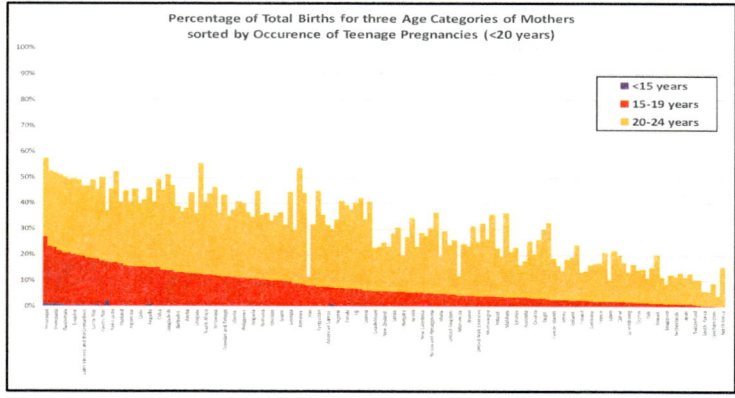

Figure 8-3: Three critical age categories for mothers as a percentage of total births[214]

[215]https://www.cia.gov/library/publications/the-world-factbook/fields/2256.html

In some countries, more than half the children are born from mothers under 25 (mainly in Latin America, Bangladesh, Azerbaijan, Armenia), whilst in some Latin American countries more than 20% of the children are born from teenage mothers. Again, it is suspected that, due to lack of African data, this is much more prevalent. In contrast, in Europe and East Asia almost all children are born from mothers older than 25 years.

When it comes to fathers, data are even more scarce. The critical age categories for parental fitness are described differently: not only young age is a critical component for parental fitness, but older fathers (> 50 years) are unlike to provide much parenting in their older age nor are families with an unknown father likely to be the most stable. Figure 8-5 visualises four critical categories of fathers: unknown, >50 years, <20 years and between 20 and 25 years. The data have been sorted from the highest percentage of unknown fathers downwards.

In some countries, almost half of the children have an unknown father. Several countries have no category for unknown fathers (noteworthy the USA...) and there are only three African countries with data on the father's age at child birth. As with the data for mothers, it is therefore suspected that the age categories at risk and the 'unknown' category are much higher.

What is clear from both Figures 8-3 and 8-4 is that almost a third of the parents are either too young or, in case of fathers, too young, unknown or too old to warrant an environment, secure and stable enough to raise children.

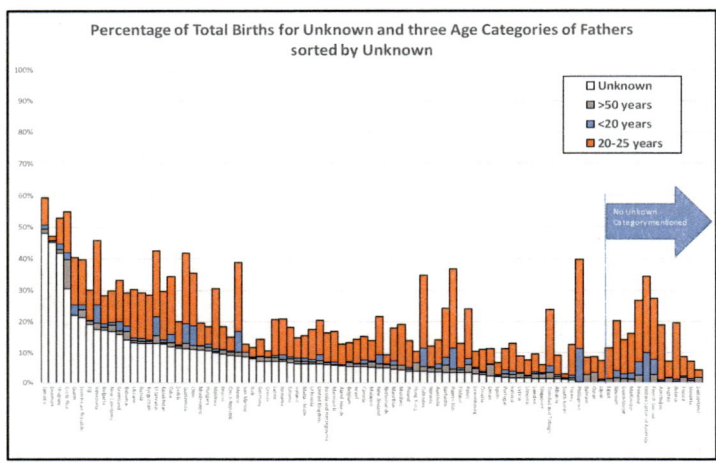

Figure 8-4: Four critical age categories for fathers as a percentage of total births[214]

With the above-mentioned limits, an age fitness matrix can be constructed, where the age of the mother and father are cross-plotted (see Figure 8-5). Ages less than 15 are left blank and ages above 50 are greyed out. The teenage years are coloured red to indicate that it is not OK to have parental responsibilities before 20 years. The age group 20–25 years has been coloured orange to show that parenthood can only start responsibly above the age of 25.

Raising one or more children on one's own is harder than when sharing the burden with a partner or an extended family, in particular in poverty situations. When neither a partner nor an extended family is present, the child is generally more susceptible to neglect, more at risk when the single parent is ill or is fired from work. In this context, I therefore do not understand the state sponsorship of IVF treatment for deliberately single mothers and I feel that this treatment should be financially subsidised for couples only (both heterosexual or homosexual). It is understandable that women want to be empowered to make their own choices,[216] but why create another child in less ideal situations? Maybe these women need to consider adoption first of all, since children without parents or with problematic parents are worse off than with a capable single parent.

Parental Age Fitness Matrix

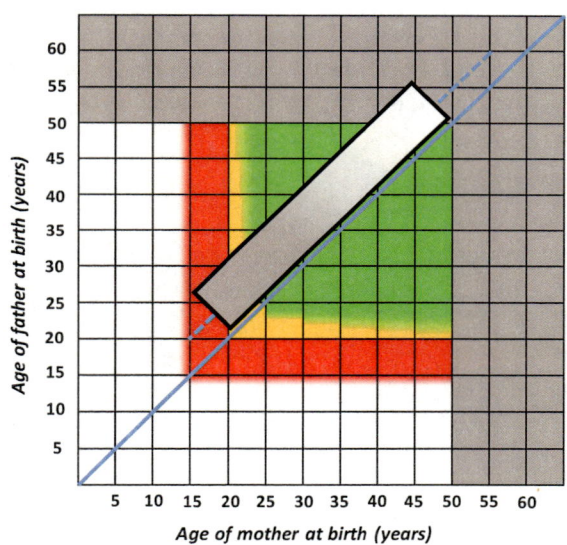

Figure 8-5: The Parental Age Fitness Matrix: the most desirable area is having parents between 25 and 50 years at birth (green area). The dashed line reflects the fact that fathers are in general around 5 years older than mothers. The rectangle around this dashed line is the area where most age combinations take place between couples. The shading in the bottom part of this rectangle represents the majority of births.

Another consideration for parental fitness is mental and physical health. In the western world, physical health is dealt with by a doctor's visit: no point starting a family when one of the

_____

[216]http://www.telegraph.co.uk/women/womens-life/11799007/IVF-The-rise-of-the-new-Solo-Mum.html

parents is seriously ill or has a genetic disease. Due to poverty or cultural bias, this is less obvious however in the developing world. Mental health of a prospective parent is often overlooked or ignored. While extensive screening takes place for people working with children (teachers, childcare), it is non-existent for parents and a significant proportion of children ends up with depressed, drunken, violent or sexually abusive parents from birth onwards. It is telling that 68% of women and 57% of men with a mental illness in the UK are parents.[217] Without sliding on the slippery slope of eugenics, it is worthwhile considering educating ill prospective parents thoroughly on the difficulties of bringing up children.

There is also evidence that parenthood itself can cause illness. The most well-known is post-natal depression of a new mother. It is estimated that between 10 and 15% of mothers suffer from this after childbirth.[218] And fathers can feel overwhelmed too by the new situation of being a parent. Both parents may be tired and stressed out with all that parental care on top of busy professional lives, in particular when societal pressures demand very responsible parents. Especially among middle-class parents, children increasingly are expected to be the centre of family life. This causes an increase in multi-tasking and only adds to the parental stress.

The fitness to raise children can also be questioned by environmental circumstances, such as alcoholism, drug addiction or inhabiting war-torn areas. These situations are not the best circumstances to procreate and raise children. Addiction to drugs and alcohol severely hampers a child's development[219] during pregnancy and can cause severe neglect or abuse of a child when growing up. War parents may be subject to casualties, physical violence, torture or rape, which could cause traumas, whilst raising children. Prior to raising children, help should be provided

[217]http://www.rcpsych.ac.uk/healthadvice/parentsandyouthinfo/parentscarers/parentalmentalillness.aspx
[218]http://www.rcpsych.ac.uk/healthadvice/problemsdisorders/postnataldepression.aspx
[219] http://www.nacoa.net/pdfs/addicted.pdf

to these prospective parents to heal them from addictions and traumas and by providing them shelter and security. Children are better off to be raised in more stable environment. This is often easier said than done, however.

Parental Responsibility

Responsibility for children is a serious business. A child's development and happiness are at stake and without responsible parents a child is unsafe and subject to neglect, abuse or bullying. In recent times the awareness of neglect, abuse or bullying and its influence on child development is better understood. Every parent wishes the best for their children and therefore parenting got better, but also has become a bigger task.

In the past, when families were bigger, children were often left on their own, lightly supervised by elder siblings or peers. The street, where most of them were playing, has not become a more dangerous place: we only have become more aware of the potential dangers. Children hanging out in the streets with only the slightest supervision is still much the situation in sub-Saharan Africa. In defence, it is often heard, that it is not only the parents who raise a child. An oft-quoted African saying is: "*It takes a village to raise a child.*"[220] This is also heard from India where indigenous fathers claim that: "*A child is the responsibility of the community.*"[221]

'What does raising children mean?' and 'who is raising children?' become rather blurred concepts in these situations and seem odd for western ears. A lot of these differences can be attributed to the presence of an extended family. But extended families are waning, despite efforts to maintain these in urban circumstances. Due to space and costs it is less economic to let extended families live in cities. The next best thing, a circle of friends or acquaintances from the same area, ethnicity or religion, is already in place in many cases both in the same country (e.g.

---

[220]http://www.incultureparent.com/2011/05/african-parenting-the-sane-way-to-raise-children/

[221]http://sowf.s3.amazonaws.com/wp-content/uploads/2015/06/08181421/State-of-the-Worlds-Fathers_23June2015.pdf Page 67.

Scottish social clubs in England) as amongst immigrants or expatriates.

Extended families have a moral obligation towards each other, albeit it less than the core family. So, responsibility towards nieces, nephews, cousins or grandchildren is taken for granted. In tribal circumstances, such as an African or Indian village, there is a smooth transition between extended family and friends/acquaintances, due to the many family bonds existing in such circumstances. Friends and acquaintances in a village keep an eye on all the children, although their responsibility for those children is relatively minimal (see Figure 8-6 left). These types of arrangements can be ideal to raise a large number of children.

With more and more people moving towards urban areas, the situation changes. Without the presence of an extended family, there is more pressure on the parents. Raising children in the rural 'African' or 'Indian' way, therefore becomes nostalgic and idyllic, since those times are either long gone (e.g. in the western world) or disappearing. Although a circle of friends and acquaintances will be present in an urban setting, they cannot be relied on as much as a member of an extended family.

This creates a gap in the caring system for the children (see Figure 8-6 right) and is often filled up by paid carers (nannies, babysitters) or by inviting an elderly grandparent into the core family. The gap in the caring system for people, who have left the traditional tribal environment is an important driver to reduce the number of children of a core family.

To carry responsibility for children professionally as a child carer, is taken seriously in the western world. It requires a couple of years training and the number of children per care worker is limited (although numbers vary a lot per country, see figure 1 of ref. 211). With required training and legal limits to child numbers, professional child care becomes expensive. In absence of an extended family, this economic consideration is a key driver to reduce the number of children per couple.

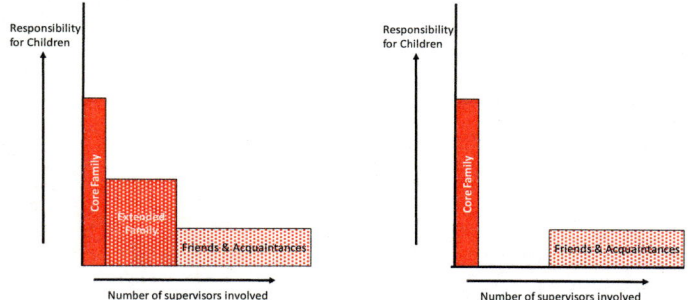

Figure 8-6: Responsibility in a tribal village (left) and a core family moving to a city without an extended family (right). Outside the core family, the responsibility for the children declines, whilst the number of supervisors increases. The gap caused by the absence of an extended family in a city, is the main driver to reduce the number of children per couple.

There are also legal implications for parental responsibility. As the most essential roles of parental responsibility, the British government identifies to provide a home for the child and to protect and maintain a child.[222] Procreating in war or hunger situations needs some careful considerations, since protection and food security cannot be guaranteed. And there is a severity scale involved: "If a child being exposed to danger is bad, then presumably two children being exposed to danger is worse and three is worse still."[223] The morality of having children and having many children will be further discussed in Chapter 10.

Can One Afford to Have a Lot of Children?

It is well known that raising a child cost a lot of money and a lot of people underestimate these costs. A typical child in the UK costs more than £230,000 (2016) to raise from birth to the age of

---

[222]https://www.gov.uk/parental-rights-responsibilities/what-is-parental-responsibility

[223] *Toward a Small Family Ethic.* Travis N. Rieder (2016), Springer Briefs in Public Health. Page 37.

21 and only with state school education[224,225] (see Figure 8-7). This is rising dramatically if the child will go to private education or boarding school.

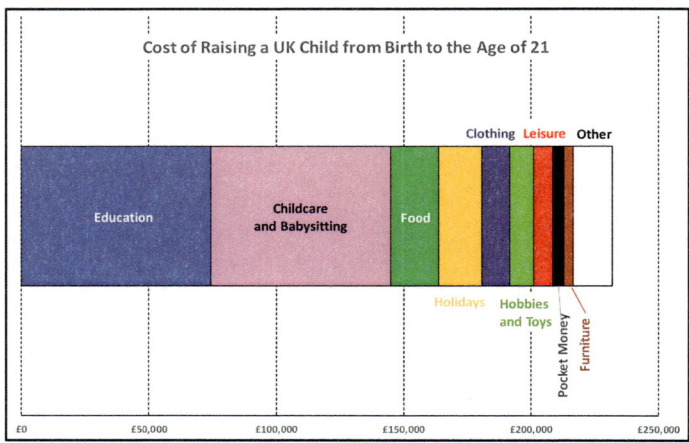

Figure 8-7: Typical cost of raising a child in the UK from birth to the age of 21 in 2016[224]

These amounts are not dissimilar in other countries: in the US, average costs are quoted to amount $ 305,000, adjusted for projected inflation (some £200,000) for a child born in 2013 till the age of 18.[226] Estimates from Belgium amounted to € 220,000 (£ 190,000) for a child born in 2014 till the age of 25[227] and from France[228] (€700 per month or €176,000 (£ 152,000) till the age of 21, born in 2011) are the same order of magnitude.

[224] Costs were compiled by the Centre of Economic and Business Research (CEBR) for LV= in December 2015

[225] The differential costs for housing does not seem to be included.

[226]http://www.huffingtonpost.com/2014/08/18/cost-of-raising-a-child_n_5688179.html

[227]http://www.demorgen.be/tvmedia/kind-opvoeden-is-even-duur-als-een-ferrari-bfa45302/

[228]http://www.la-croix.com/Actualite/France/Ce-que-coute-un-enfant-2015-06-30-1329614

Even in the developing world costs are relatively high ($82,000 in India till the age of 21[229] (2011)) is high in relation to average annual earnings. People in the developing world are beginning to realise this, as the following examples indicate:

- The majority of Indian parents start saving for raising and educating their child, when the child is less than 3 years, although 37% think it is a struggle to fund their children's long-term needs.[230]
- In some urban areas in China where the one-child policy has been relaxed and permission has been given to have more than one child, families still choose to have only one — largely because of economic uncertainty (from ref. 208).
- *"People used to want six or seven or even 12 children, but nobody can do that now. It's the economics. It costs a lot to raise a child."* Nigerian mother of four.[231]

It is a disgrace that, because of economic hardship, the poorest people in particular can hardly afford children. But the poorest still have children, hence the start of massive inequality. And this whilst some rich people seem to use children as way to show off their wealth, instead of giving an example to the rest of the country that overpopulation affects everybody. With the omnipresence of television, internet and newspapers, people look up at celebrities and statesmen as role models. British high-profile characters like Tony and Cherie Blair (5), Boris and Marina Johnson (4), David and Victoria Beckham (4) or Jamie and Jools Oliver (5) definitely give off the wrong message and create envy for people unable to afford so many children. There are moral obligations towards a smaller number of children in the western world and people in the

---

[229] https://en.wikipedia.org/wiki/Cost_of_raising_a_child
[230]http://economictimes.indiatimes.com/which-investment-option-is-the-best-for-your-childs-future/estimate-the-cost-of-raising-your-child/slideshow/8007024.cms
[231]http://www.nytimes.com/2012/04/15/world/africa/in-nigeria-a-preview-of-an-overcrowded-planet.html?_r=0

limelight should accept that they are role models for a larger society.

And then there are environmental considerations. Calculations have been made to calculate the impact of a new born American child: excluding the effect of further generations, each American child adds about 9441 metric tonne of CO_2 over a lifetime. This is 5.7 times the average lifetime emissions of an American woman in non-procreative activities.[232] Having less or no children is the greenest thing one can do. Note that worldwide we are in 'ecological overshoot': globally, we currently consume resources at a rate of 1.6 planets per year (i.e. it takes the world 1.6 year to regenerate what we use in a year).[233] And if everybody would live like a US citizen, we would consume even more planets!

Having discussed overpopulation from the perspective of children and adults, it is now time to do the same for the old age cohort, since they are a rapidly growing part of our population.

---

[232]https://digginginthedriftless.com/2011/04/29/our-carbon-legacy-and-our-kids/ I must admit that I do not fully understand the 5.7 multiplier, since it would suggest that a new-born would consume 5.7 times more over his/her lifetime than the current generation, which seem excessive.

[233]http://www.footprintnetwork.org/en/index.php/GFN/page/world_footprint/

Chapter 9
We Are Getting Older – Can We Afford It and Do We Want It?

An Increasing Life Expectancy: The Road to Immortality?

Because of improved hygiene and medical advances, life expectancy has been rising steadily since the 19th century (see Chapter 2). And recently average global life expectancy is rising very fast with an increase of 5 years between 2000 and 2015.[234] In advanced economies, life expectancy has been increasing at 2.5 years every decade (or 6 hours every day).[235] In the UK, it currently stands at 79 years for a man and almost 83 years for a woman at birth. But once one has reached the age of 65, one can expect to live even longer: more than 83 years for a man and almost 86 years for a woman (see Figure 9-1).

Greg Lee Carter in his book *Population and Society* mentions three different causes for death. In 2012, 23% of the world population died of contagious diseases (red shades in Figure 9-2), 68% from non-contagious diseases (blue shades in Figure 9-2) and only 9% from Injuries and Suicide (grey shades in Figure 9-2).[236]

---

[234]http://www.who.int/gho/mortality_burden_disease/life_tables/situation_tr ends_text/en/

[235] *How Population Change Will Transform Our World*, Sarah Harper. Oxford University Press (2016) p. 59

[236] *Population and Society* by Gregg Lee Carter. Polity Press (2016) Table 3.2.

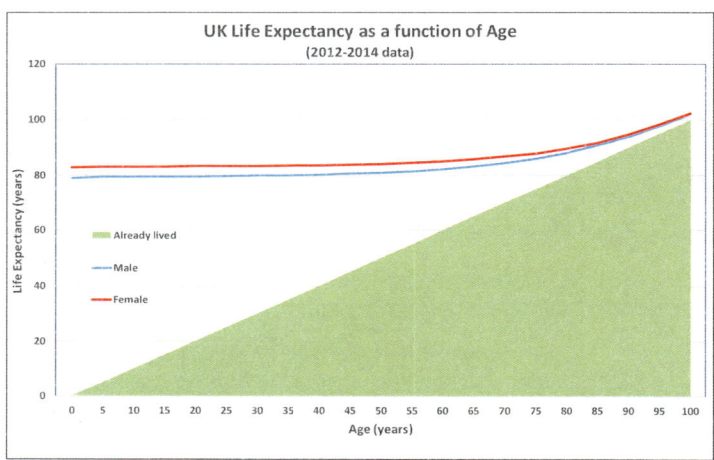

Figure 9-1: UK life expectancy as a function of age.[237] Note the increase once one has lived up to 60–65 years.

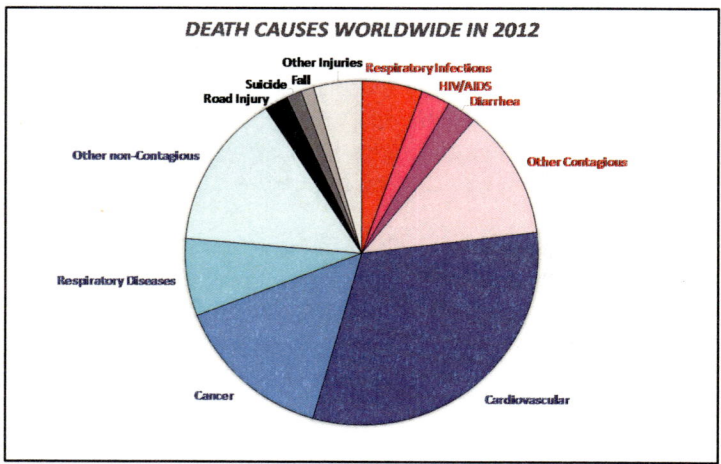

Figure 9-2: Worldwide death causes: Contagious Diseases (23%), red/purple shades, Non-contagious Diseases (68%), blue shades and Injuries/Suicide (9%), black/grey shades

[237] Data from: http://www.riskprediction.org.uk/index_lifeexp.php

Due to an aggressive inoculation programme and improved hygiene in the developing nations, it is expected that death by contagious disease will fall dramatically this century. The main causes of death in the world are cardiovascular diseases (almost one third). But these types of diseases are also waning in the more developed countries because of a healthier diet and lifestyle. Progress is made in cancer treatments by either postponing or curing the illness. Thus, death is postponed on a large scale resulting in an increase in life expectancy.

Where will this stop? Progress in medical science is rapid and we are at the onset of the use of gene therapy at a much larger scale to combat genetic diseases and Alzheimer. Prosthetics are undergoing a revolution and we may become part organic, part non-organic. Another development is the growing of replacement organs from stem cells, which could be used to replace worn-out organs. Combatting the aging process is ongoing everywhere and some authors[238] are convinced that we will reach immortality reasonably soon. This results in several questions:

1. Can a hybrid person, equipped with non-organic body parts and potentially supplemented with artificial intelligence still be called Homo sapiens? This will be discussed at the end of the next chapter.
2. Can everybody afford all the medical improvements? Even now we wonder where the limits are to supply free but (very) expensive medication as part of the British NHS. And AIDS medication is not affordable for everybody at the current market prices. The inequality of the pension situation will be discussed in the next section.
3. Do we want to live longer or become immortal? Under the current circumstances there is a substantial gap between morbidity and mortality. What will the quality of life be at very old age? A lot of older people are already tired of life due to monotony, loneliness, aggravated by physical disabilities and dire financial circumstances. This is discussed in the final two sections.

---

[238] *Homo Deus: A Brief History of Tomorrow*, Yuval Harari (2016), Harvill Seeker.

Pensions and Can We Afford Them for Everyone?

The idea that population should grow, was not solely promoted by the elites, who wanted a large enough workforce to work the land or to labour in their factories. Genuine demographic worries exist, which are underlain by naivety and ignorance. A lot of us seem very worried that the demographic pyramid is inverting and that there will be more retirees than workers. Even when this would occur, it is likely to be temporarily and is offset by an increase in pension age, which is already underway in a lot of countries. The population pyramid will be inverted when the population is shrinking (TFR less than the replacement ratio of 2.1). During the transition towards a smaller population, it is important that the pyramid will not invert too much, since this might create instability: when the working cohorts can no longer carry the financial burden of maintaining the older cohorts and/or when the quality of life of older cohorts is dropping dramatically (see Figure 9-3).

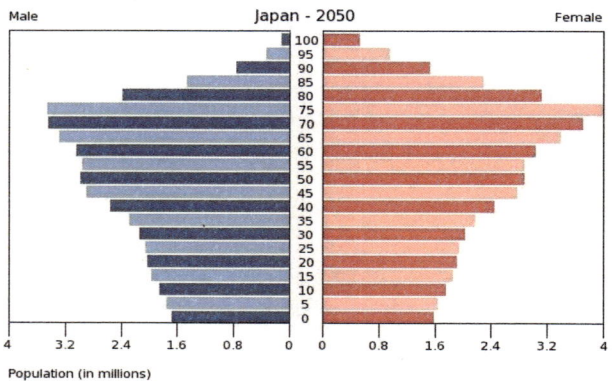

Figure 9-3: Japan's population pyramid by 2050.[239] The old age dependency ratio will increase to 74% by 2050.[240] It is not clear whether this will be sustainable, unless pension age is increased. This is however already happening in many countries.

[239] http://blog-imgs-43.fc2.com/m/u/r/murakof/japan2050pyramid.jpg
[240] http://www.economist.com/node/13611235

However, the additional advantages of a shrinking population are not often mentioned: a smaller population in crowded cities will have a beneficial effect on house prices and trains and buses will become less packed. If a constant GDP in a country (provided we still maintain this crude measure of wellbeing) is maintained at the same level, the per capita numbers will rise with a shrinking population. This phenomenon is more or less happening in Japan over the last 10 years.

The fear of a percentage decline of the working age population is largely unfounded and obsolete. Due to an improved lifestyle with more and more mechanisation, shorter working hours and further advances in health care, people can work longer than 50 years ago. The definition of working age is blurring and gap years during one's professional life are common and accepted. Most countries now accept a higher pension age limit, with people working well after 65. The increase in life expectancy over the last 50 years (see Figure 2-1), implicitly means a healthier 65+ population. However, it is true that traditional state pensions relied on an age pyramid, where a larger working population supported a smaller cohort of pensioners. Due to the change in demographics, this will change: in Europe, the old age dependency ratio (the ratio of the old age cohort, generally defined as older than 65 years, divided by the working age cohort) is set to rise dramatically (see Figure 9-4).[241]

---

[241]http://www.worldbank.org/content/dam/Worldbank/Feature%20Story/ECA/ECA-Pensions-Report-2014.pdf

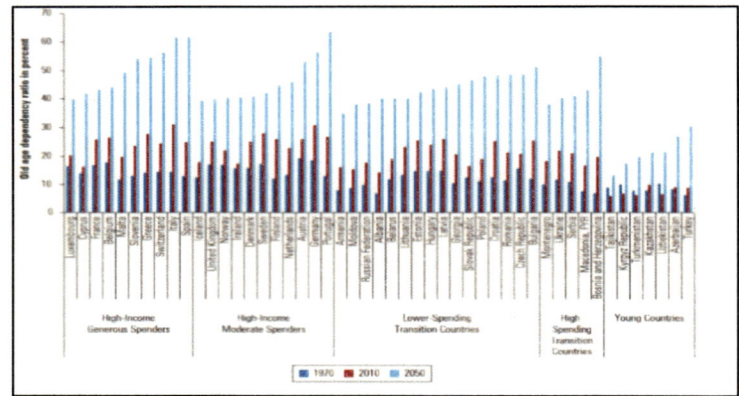

Figure 9-4: Ratio of the old-age cohort as a percentage of the working age cohort is set to increase dramatically over the next decades (ref. 239 figure 2.22).

The generous pension schemes of the later part of the 20th century were mostly a result of a '*growing population of workers, not by the generosity of benevolent politicians or by a fair return on contributions'.[242]* Traditional pension schemes need restructuring and reformation, which is already taking place in a lot of countries. More and more people are relying on savings or private pension schemes to overcome the expected shortfalls. It is also worth mentioning that pension schemes set up in the middle part of the 20th century are based on an average life expectancy of 15 years after retirement. Currently people generally live longer than 80 years (retirement age of 65 years + 15 years of life expectancy). An increase in retirement age seems therefore justified. The World Bank report is relatively optimistic about this possibility:

"If countries could now raise retirement ages until life expectancy at retirement is 15 years, as it was in the 1970s, most could afford to day's benefit structure even with the future challenging demographics. Alternatively, countries could choose

[242] Ref. 239, p. 26

to reduce benefits to a more basic level, comparable to what was provided in the 1970s, but retain the right to retire at age 65. Or they could do both, that is, raise the retirement age while reducing benefits, which would mean less drastic changes on both counts. "[243]

However, life expectancy is not the same for everyone. Unfortunately, the poorer part of the population lives significantly shorter than the richer part. In a study of the lifespan of rich and poor people in England and Wales, it was quoted that for men at the age of 30, (the probably richest) 5% of men can be expected to live till an average age of 96 years, whilst (the probably poorest) 10% of men can expect only to live until an average 62 years only.[244] Raising the pension age would disproportionate benefit the richer part of the pensioners, since a larger proportion of the poorer cohort would die before claiming the pension they have contributed to.[245]

Private pensions are also on the rise, since it is increasingly difficult to survive on state pensions only. However, in Britain over a quarter of the 55–64 years' age cohort do not have a private pension and that number is increasing more than 40% for all individuals.[246] The main reason is low wage jobs and this is likely to get worse with the increase of zero hour contracts and the gig economy. In countries like China the situation is direr, since only state pensions exist and are managed by local governments rather than nationally creating mobility barriers, whilst state pensions are only invested in Chinese government bonds and bank deposits.[247]

With increasing dependency ratios due to a shrinking population, it is likely that pensions may not be affordable for everyone. It may well be that family needs to step in again similar

[243] Ref. 239, p. 27

[244]http://www.independent.co.uk/news/uk/home-news/life-expectancy-gap-between-rich-poor-widening-first-time-in-150-years-men-women-a7010881.html

[245]https://www.theguardian.com/membership/2017/mar/29/a-world-without-retirement

[246]https://www.theguardian.com/membership/2017/jan/23/saving-retirement-pension-generation-old-age

[247]https://www.ft.com/content/d4ce82e4-937a-11e5-bd82-c1fb87bef7af

to what happened before the introduction of a pension system. In Britain already 20% of people between 50–64 years, care for their elderly parents.[248] This may increase in the future. It should be noticed however that with a shrinking population, the rising old age (>65–70 years) dependency ratio is offset by a reducing young age dependency ratio (<18 years). Financially the working age cohort should be able to share a bit more therefore. Implicitly this means however to keep the percentage investment per child constant.

And of course, funding for state pension and social care should be discussed politically. With an increasing old age cohort in many countries, one would expect increased funding for this cohort. Fortunately, this is happening,[249] but one can question whether this will be enough. Similarly, a reducing cohort of young people should see reduced budgets. However, this does not seem to happen in several western countries with a shrinking youth cohort (see Table 9-1, which highlights this over the period 1999–2012). Political spending choices need to be made to provide the old age cohort with reasonable living standards. The young have the future is the saying and they are certainly and increasingly taken care off. Alternatively, one can argue whether aging countries should invest less in defence, law and order (aging populations are less violent!), space or medical research.

---

[248]https://www.theguardian.com/membership/2017/feb/13/new-retirement-ageing-responsibility-carers-parents-children-care-crisis
[249]British data from https://www.kingsfund.org.uk
/sites/files/kf/field/field_publication_file/Spending%20on%20health%20...
%2050%20years%20low%20res%20for%20web.pdf Table 5.

Country	Part of Population < 15 years		Investment in Education (%GDP)	
	1999	2012	1999	2012
France	18.9%	18.4%	5.6%	5.5%
Germany	15.4%	13.3%	4.6%	4.9%
Japan	14.8%	13.0%	3.5%	3.8%
UK	19.2%	17.7%	4.3%	5.2%

Investment in the young stabilises or rises, despite smaller cohorts in four selected countries with a stabilised fertility rate

Table 9-1: Over a 13-year period the investment in the cohort under 15 years stabilises or increases whilst the cohort size decreases. Population data from OECD[250] and education investment data from the World Bank[251]

Quality of Life in Later Years

Currently the number of life years without disability is 1.8 years less than the life expectancy. In the future, this morbidity – mortality gap is expected to rise to 3 years in the UK.[252] And this gap is also wider for the poor. To live in a wheelchair, having to rely on others for transport or care, is reducing our quality of life significantly. This is physical health of course, but one should not exclude mental or financial health either. One may still be very healthy in old age, but isolation and constant financial worries about affordability of the last years of one's life is debasing the joy of longevity.

Apart from the very rich, old age for most people is becoming a longer and longer period of relatively poor quality of life. Families are getting smaller, are generally living further apart because the working age cohort has been moving to cities or

---

[250] Population data from: https://data.oecd.org/pop/young-population.htm#indicator-chart

[251] http://data.worldbank.org/indicator/SE.XPD.TOTL.GD.ZS. No data for Germany in 1999 and assumed the same as in 1998 (4.8%). UK data in 2012 not mentioned and back-calculated from £85 M educational budget from https://www.statista.com/statistics/298522/public-expenditure-science-and-technology-united and a 2012 GDP of £ 1675 M

[252] *How Population Change Will Transform Our World.* Sarah Harper (2016). Oxford University Press. p.87.

following work opportunities elsewhere. There is therefore an increased risk of isolation for people in the old age cohorts. Work and raising a family is often stressful and apart from a work network and family, there is little time left for a social network. This can hit extra hard after retirement, when work stops and children flee the nest, whilst no social safety net remains. In a recent UK survey, only 56% of the retirees say that they enjoy retirement a great deal and just 57% feel it is working out as they planned.[253]

Our unbridled pursuit of longevity by both public as private funding of medical research seems to take priority over the quality of our remaining years. Extending lives of both old (and young) cost an enormous amount of money and yet what are we extending? An empty and austere last 20–25 years of one's life? These are important life choices.

Reducing the world population will inevitably increase the relative size of the old age cohort, during a period of transition. But why make this cohort even bigger by promoting and prioritising longevity? A transition period with bigger old age cohorts, living meaningless lives should not be a punishment for older people.

The discussion on affordability of a good quality old age is only just beginning. This goes in parallel with the expected drop in employment due to mechanisation and robotisation. Can we afford to care for so many people, both unemployed and old? The idea of a Universal Basic Income (as discussed in Chapter 4) is therefore gaining ground. In the unequal world, we live in, it can be expected that this will be fiercely resisted. Inequality reduction is however not only key to a fairer humane world, but also very important to reduce population in a smooth and dignified way.

The quantity of years versus quality of life debate should be discussed more openly: some people want a better quality of life but do not want to live so long. Can this choice be realised? This brings us to the last section.

---

[253]https://www.theguardian.com/membership/2017/mar/06/how-to-retire-successfully-you-need-to-ask-what-you-want-out-of-life

Transition: Suicide and Euthanasia?

At first glance suicide seems like a terrible thing to propose, human beings normally cling to life. However, transitioning to a smaller world population, actively or as result of an already dropping fertility rate, is not a particular normal situation: we never experienced a situation like this before in human history. If inequality stays as it is or increases, when the rich refuse to share with the poorer or older cohorts, the quality of life of these cohorts will be very much reduced. Suicide and euthanasia are therefore a way out of a (very) poor quality of life. Especially older people without children are susceptible for a potential suicide option. They realise that care is becoming so expensive that a lot of people fall back to family help. A recent article in the Guardian[254] quotes for the UK that:

There are one million over-65s without adult children in the UK, a figure expected to double by 2030. The data does not include people who are without their children because of bereavement, estrangement, distance or any other reason.

And the same article quotes an older couple (Mr and Mrs Allen):

Without children of their own, the Allens are looking at every way they can think of to avoid a 'long, drawn-out period of anguish at the end of our lives'. This includes euthanasia. The couple are devastatingly clear about the choices that lie ahead of them. "What prompted our interest in euthanasia is that we don't have children," he said. "We're having to look at all the options ... because we don't have anyone to put us first."

People should have a choice to end their own life, how terrible or sad this may be. Deaths by suicide were 1.4% of the world population in 2012 (see reference of Figure 9-2) and global suicide rates have risen 60% over the last 45 years.[255] Unfortunately, suicide is still a taboo and medication is therefore not available, since it implicates drug companies, doctors and chemists in the

[254]https://www.theguardian.com/membership/2017/feb/13/new-retirement-ageing-responsibility-carers-parents-children-care-crisis
[255]http://www.suicide.org/international-suicide-statistics.html

same way as euthanasia. Too many people end their lives in a terrible way by hanging or throwing themselves under a train, causing distress for many others. Euthanasia and assisted suicide is only legal in a very limited amount of developed countries, whilst most of the developing world has no legal system on these issues in place.

An austere life may instigate a revolt of poorer and older people against an iron grip of the rich elites. But alternatively, people might not want to live under these conditions and prefer to opt for suicide. To get rid of the financial 'burden' of the poor and old may in fact suit the rich elite and 'humane' suicide options might even be actively promoted by them. This seems a grim dystopian future but not altogether unrealistic. It reminds of the eugenics era in Nazi Germany and the 1930s sterilisation laws in the US. From an ethical perspective, it is thus understandable that suicide medication is not so readily available and only limited to the terminally ill, who, unbiased, see no quality of life left for them. Again, this dilemma highlights the need to vigorously decrease inequality first.

Chapter 10
Ethics and a Look into the Future

What Is Enough?

If we freeze technological developments to the developments of today, we are clearly consuming more than our planet can sustain in the long run. In the near term, hunger can be eradicated, since so much food is wasted and so many obese people in the western world can do with less food. But we forget that to provide sufficient food for everybody we have to rely on industrialised agriculture, which is far from being sustainable. The area of tropical rainforest is reducing every year to accommodate growth in food consumption. This cannot go on for ever.

Consumption per capita, in particular in the developed world, needs to come down. But on the other hand, a large part of the people in the developing nations live in abject poverty. We have a moral duty to lift the developing nations out of this poverty. However, by doing so, consumption per capita in the developing world will rise, which will in turn put pressure on a sustainable planet. This seems the ultimate contradiction in terms, until we start to look at populations. To achieve a sustainable planet, both consumption and energy use in the western world needs to come down dramatically and fertility rates for both the developed and developing world needs to be reduced, but more strongly for the developing world.

Addressing the sustainability of our planet without discussing future innovations, seems incomplete. It is hard to predict even the near future, since changes occur very rapidly (25 years ago, there was barely Internet). And yet while discussing future innovations, we need to be careful not to extrapolate too much. History has taught us that innovations go stepwise and not in a continuous line. Due to the improved connectivity of the ever-increasing influence of the Internet, the recent trend of discoveries and innovations is impressive, but some caution is warranted. Politicians can put brakes on innovative measures to stop climate change, because of short-termism caused by elections taking place every four or five years. For example, lobbying has resulted in maintaining indirect subsidies and tax breaks for coal and oil companies in the UK, whilst government incentives for household solar capacity are reduced.[256] However, some authors remain very optimistic on the solar conversion from fossil fuels.[257]

Future sustainability is already harder to grasp. If we limit ourselves to an anthropocentric definition of sustainability as 'enough to provide energy and feed mankind', we may be able to get over the expected population maximum of 11 billion by the end of the century. But what life will this be? A life full of inequality, poverty, wars, climate change effects and barely any nature left to enjoy? Other species will clearly suffer by increasing the already vast areas of monoculture or as domesticated animals, destined to a miserable life, providing us with meat and dairy products. Don't we have an obligation of stewardship for the planet? Considering biodiversity, animal welfare and planetary limits, we already live unsustainably. Future increases in population will only increase this unsustainability. To live sustainable as a species on this planet requires major changes.

I read Bill McKibben's book *The End of Nature*,[258] just after becoming a father of my second child. The book is a passionate plea for the beauty of the natural world and what 'civilisation' had done to it. For me it was a moment to reflect on procreation, just as Bill McKibben did with his later book *Maybe One*[259] after the birth of his daughter. Maintaining nature's biodiversity is not only important to us to keep our planet in a sound ecological balance,

---

[256]https://www.theguardian.com/environment/2016/apr/08/solar-installation-in-british-homes-falls-by-three-quarters-after-subsidy-cuts

[257] *The Switch: How Solar, Storage and New Tech Means Cheap Power for All.* Chris Goodall, Profile Books

[258] *The End of Nature.* Bill McKibben. Viking Books (1990)

[259] *Maybe One.* Bill McKibben. Anchor books (1999).

the richness of nature also provides us with pleasure, relaxation and for some a degree of spirituality.

We use various ways to address sustainability. The first way is complete denial ('après moi, le deluge') or at its mildest engagement not to look further than one's own life. Unfortunately, quite a lot of people in the western world live like that, in particular when money is not a constraint (The hedonistic lifestyle of some billionaires or millionaires speaks for itself). But how far into the future should we aim with our sustainable efforts? There is a danger of solely living in the future and constantly worrying about what could happen. Often these worriers do not incorporate potential future technological developments and extrapolate purely from the past and present. In my opinion it is best to focus on the timeframe of one to two generations (25–50 years) and adapt our actions accordingly. Most of us have children or grandchildren and do we not all want the best for them?

Herman Daly in his book on *Steady State Economics* quotes mathematician Georgescu-Roegen[260] by saying that '*the human species should have a lifespan as long as it is compatible with its dowry of low entropy*'. Therefore, the utilitarian principle of the 'Greatest Good for the Greatest Number' (Bentham) seems an impossible double maximisation. Georgescu-Roegen proposes to change this into a '*Sufficient Good Life*' (rather than Greatest Good) for the '*Cumulative Number of Human Beings*' (rather than the Greatest Number). And cumulative means from the very start of mankind, since we are benefitting from the planet by increasing entropy. This cumulative number of human beings therefore cannot be an infinite amount since each person needs a minimum amount of entropy to live from, whilst the world's resources are finite.

Enough people should also be linked to a meaningful life for everybody. Enough should not mean the current status quo, where almost three billion people live on less than $2 per day; where around one billion is illiterate and where one billion have no access to clean and safe water. These numbers will only rise in the future under a 'status quo' scenario. It is therefore important to

---

[260] H. Daly, *Steady State Economics*, Island Press, second edition (1991), p.207.

link 'enough' people to a minimum living standard. Equality amongst human beings is one of the most difficult subjects. As a species, we always have been unequal although relative wealth is more important than absolute wealth. Greed and resulting inequality seem part of our existence. However, should there be no limits? Why aim for a billionaire? Is to be a millionaire not enough? And even that…

Right to Have as Many Children as One Desires?

In her excellent book *One Child, do we have a Right to More?*[261], Sarah Corly discusses extensively the sticky points around the right to have children. The United Nations Declaration of Human Rights states that we have a moral right to procreate, but does not mention anything on the number of children one can have. Corly rightly introduces an analogy that '*citizens have a right to food, but this is not taken to be a right to Roman banquets every night*'.[262]

One strong argument she is using that rights cannot be cast in stone forever, since conditions change over time. For example, when the Declaration of Human Rights were drafted, we could not have foreseen the influence overpopulation would have on biodiversity or climate change. Does this mean we need to stick to our rights and do nothing about this? In particular, religions are dragging their feet and are the last ones to change (e.g. contraception ban in the Catholic Church): quite telling is that the saying 'cast in stone' comes from the Bible, when God chiselled the Ten Commandments for Moses to distribute. In biblical times, it was probably good to procreate enough offspring, since a lot of children died and people had no other provisions for old age than to rely on their children. Due to infant mortality, hunger, sickness and wars, the world population was kept in check and fairly stable for thousands of years. Times have changed drastically and

---

[261] *One Child, Do We Have a Right to More?* Sarah Corly (2016) Oxford University Press
[262] Ibid. p. 18

conservatism and its adage of 'cast in stone' are no longer suitable solutions for the problems of today.

Some people seem unfamiliar (or stubborn…) with the facts that we live in a dynamic world, where changes occur. Habits, cultures and religions all change: no one would condone cannibalism or burning of witches anymore. Most of us now condemn the death penalty or FGM, whilst the rights of homosexual people are accepted by more and more people these days. With changes in habits and cultures, also rights change. Corly quotes Nobel Prize winner, Amartya Sen, regarding the right to reproduce: *"Despite the importance of reproductive rights, if their existence were to generate disasters such as massive misery and hunger, then we would have to question whether they deserve full protection."*[263]

Corly is a strong advocate for one child only per woman. She reasons that most of us have an urge to procreate and to experience parenthood. It is therefore understandable that people may lack meaning in life without raising any children. But after having one child, it becomes less justifiable to have another one. Travis Rieder claims that in this light, to have no child might be a kind of a tragedy; but being 'forced' having only one child cannot be justified as a tragedy.[264]

Corly distinguishes three types of claims, people are making regarding reproductive rights:

- *The urge to continue the family lineage.* However, one child should be enough to do this. Some people only want to make sure that a male heir is born to the family. We all know the classic story of King Henry VIII, but even in recent days this 'right' persists. This seems very sexist in our days of gender equality and should not form the basis of a right to reproduce without limits. It becomes a bit trickier, when the first born proved to be a physically or mentally disabled child. It is true that disabled children can also provide parents with love and meaning in their

---

[263] Ibid. p. 89

[264] *Toward a Small Family Ethic.* Travis N. Rieder (2016), Springer Briefs in Public Health. Pages 47–48.

life. However, I can also see that parents want to have another healthy child to ensure that both the disabled sibling as themselves will have some care in later years. Despite all the good care which is around for handicapped (or older) people in the western world and despite the potential existence of strained family relationships, blood bonds are considered invaluable by many people. In the case of disability, Corly also agrees that there could be situations where '*no normal person would find the relationship rewarding*'[265] and that the desire to have another child is fully justified.

- *The urge to have a family life.* The value of family life does not depend on the number of children in the family. Quality does not depend on quantity.[266] The family life of the seven children of the Von Trapp family in *The Sound of Music* is completely romanticised. Cosiness in a family can also be obtained by one or two children with or without visiting friends. And where is the limit: do four children provide a better family life than a two-child family? Or is an eight-child family better than a four-child family?[267] The uniqueness of every child and the consequent variety in children's characters is no right in itself to have a limitless family size.

- *The urge to have the same number of children or more children as someone else* (Corly calls this equality). This could be relevant if one has no children: 'the only worth of a woman is to be a mother' and 'I am man enough to fill a pram' are two sayings reflecting societal pressure to procreate. Even today urging couples to have children is much alive, even if that would involve costly and painful IVF. This standing in society seems from another era, until you see in the press pictures of celebrities with their large families (see Figure 10-1). These pictures seem to tell: look at me, I made it, I can afford a big happy family!

---

[265] *One Child, Do We Have a Right to More?* Sarah Corly (2016) Oxford University Press, p.58
[266] Ibid. p.50
[267] Ibid. p.51

Having a big family turns into a status symbol and can create envy for other people, unable to afford such a large family. For a man, this pride and standing seems to have been scaled by Genghis Khan, who according to folklore, sired between 3000 and 4000 children. Polygamist and president of South Africa, Jacob Zuma also falls into this category, being a father of at least 22 children. Societal pressure, showing off wealth or primitive pride are however no reasons to claim the right to have an unbounded family size.

Figure 10-1: A celebrity chef showing off his large family.[268] A new status symbol?

And what would happen if the proposal to have small families clashes with other rights? Since Corly's book is written for the American market, she has a lengthy debate over the clash with religious rights.[269] However religious rights cannot be all encompassing and in most countries secular law surpasses religious dogmas. Contraception (Catholic Church) and abortion stances made by religious groups must obey the laws made by a democratic representation of the people of a country. So, if the

---

[268] Photo courtesy of PA Images.
[269] Ibid. p.78-87

proposal for small families gets solidified into a law or as an excessive children's tax, this needs to be abided by everyone. As with religious 'rights', democratic laws and regulation take precedence over cultural prejudices and corresponding entitlements of large families.

A more socio-ethical stance is proposed by Herman Daly in his book *Steady State Economics* over which right gets priority: *"The minimum requirement of people already born should take precedence over the population reproductive desires in excess of replacement, or less than the replacement birth rate, if the existing population is considered too large."*[270] This contemplation is particular relevant in areas where hunger, war or droughts prevail. Reproductive desires driven by patriarchy or security for old age, should not take priority over more pressing matters. And besides, it is time to put patriarchal desires aside anyway.

Some libertarians may argue that imposing a law or extra taxes to deal with the subject of large families, will be yet another example of government intervention into one's private life and intrusion into one's home. However, this 'intrusion' already exists for cases of spousal and child neglect or abuse. After some initial protests, we have adjusted to these new laws and regulations and the vast majority of us agree.[271]

Duties Not Rights

In the discussion of overpopulation versus climate change, Travis Rieder does not talk about rights but he feels we have *duties* towards each other. He is mentioning three important duties:[272]

1. *A duty not to harm others.* Everyone using fossil fuels contributes to global warming with consequent changes in climatic patterns and sea level rise. This is harmful for people living in places at risk, which are often different

[270] H. Daly, *Steady State Economics*, Island Press, second edition, p.48.
[271] *One Child, Do We Have a Right to More?* Sarah Corly (2016) Oxford University Press, p. 105.
[272] *Toward a Small Family Ethic*. Travis N. Rieder (2016), Springer Briefs in Public Health. Pages 26–36.

from where the bulk of the damage is created (e.g. the Maldives are destined to drown caused by the action of others). We have some personal duty as human beings not to hurt anybody else. Increased population will increase harm. Personally, I would like to extend this concept of harm to the animal world as well.

2. *A duty of justice towards the poorest of us.* Climate change hits the poorest countries harder. This is increasing inequality. Westerners with a high-energy consumption are therefore responsible for a rising inequality in the world.

3. *Obligation towards our own children.* People with high energy consumption or in overpopulated areas, leave a desolate planet (depleted, hotter and with limited biodiversity) for our offspring.

Discouraging people to have many children is not the same as discouraging people to have no children. Addressing rich philandering pop-stars, rich polygamist presidents as well poor African peasants to reduce their offspring to levels sustainable for the planet, is providing the same norm for everybody. In that respect, I feel it is morally just to impose this also on African poorer people. Africans hardly can be held responsible for climate change, due to their very small carbon footprint, but to imply that they are therefore exempt from responsible procreation, is not very well thought through (see opinions of Naomi Klein, listed in footnote 10 (Chapter 1) and George Monbiot).[273] In the previous chapters, I have given many reasons to limit procreation. Climate change is only one of them and the discussion of smaller families should be held beyond this subject.[274]

On poverty, Travis Rieder mentions that it is our '*duty of justice to pull out some of the world's poorest out of poverty thus*

---

[273] *How Did We Get into This Mess?* George Monbiot (2016), Verso Books, Chapter 18.
[274] I have noticed the same limitation in the ethical books of Sarah Corly (*One Child*) and Travis Rieder (*Toward a Small Family Ethic*), referenced earlier.

increasing their resource consumption'.[275] This needs to happen concurrently with population control, which will further reduce poverty and inequality (see Figures 2-6 and 4-4 for the strong links). An increase in consumption in the developing nations will be adding stress to climate change, food production and use of minerals, but this is morally just. But a reduced fertility rate and a potential rapid change to renewable energy (solar energy really works in Africa!) could offset the worries over increased consumption in the developing world. Also, population control is something a poorer country can decide itself, whilst help from others to reduce poverty may be seen as paternalistic.

Parental Fitness

Sarah Corly avoids the question of parental fitness by claiming that *'licensing parents makes a differentiation that is too likely to allow prejudice'* and therefore allows one child for everyone.[276] However, in real life we are already judging who can have children and who cannot. An obvious example is severely mentally disabled people, who are completely unfit for child-rearing. We also license adoptive parents with a number of requirements, which not everybody meets. There are quite a lot of us, who would support chemical castration of paedophiles and should we allow drug addicts or alcoholics to procreate? Children of addicts have a high chance of neglect and abuse, whilst their child-raising burden falls indirectly on society as a whole. Best to get over one's addiction first. Some other voices mention 'do not procreate when you cannot afford it financially'. The financial independence is common sense, but can also be interpreted as 'leave procreation to the rich'.[277] The latter is grossly unfair: the poor are already punished by their living standards; deprivation of

---

[275] *Toward a Small Family Ethic.* Travis N. Rieder (2016), Springer Briefs in Public Health. Page 2.

[276] *One Child, Do We Have a Right to More?* Sarah Corly (2016) Oxford University Press, p.55

[277] Some of the elite (Boris Johnson (4), the late Duke of Westminster (4), Tony Blair (5)), some celebrities (David Beckham (4), Jamie Oliver (5) Gordon Ramsay (5)) and some philandering pop-stars (Mick Jagger (8!), Rod Stewart (8!), Paul Weller (5)) have executed this adage in practice

children could make the life of poor people meaningless, robotic and evolving only around subsistence. Arguments like this are reminiscent of selective breeding strategies (e.g. eugenics laws in Nazi Germany or sterilisation laws in the USA in the 1930s). The decision on who is allowed children and who is not, is like a slippery slope ending in eugenics (see Figure 10-2). Most of us stop somewhere along the slope and fortunately very few make it to the bottom. Some of decisions are generally accepted, others differ from person to person.

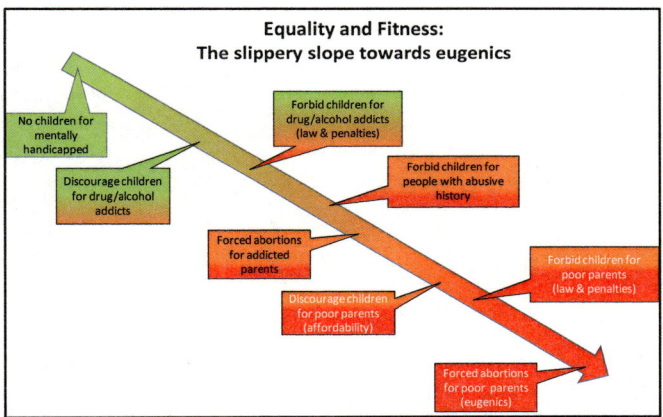

Figure 10-2: Who is fit to parent? Some examples along a slippery slope towards Eugenics

Tolerance

We should not forget that our species is a highly social one, but we are not all equal. Throughout history, we have always lived with inequality. Although we are highly adaptable, it can be questioned how much we can and should tolerate. Whilst the Christian inquisition roared in the medieval Europe, places like Cordoba, Istanbul and Cairo were havens of religious tolerance. Coexistence of cultures is a good thing to have, since it promotes tolerance and respect. Unfortunately, one culture is often dominating the other, causing frictions. Not everything within a culture should be considered sacrosanct either and cultural entitlement should not be allowed, else we would still be living with cannibalism, burning of witches or slavery. Cultures are not forever and can change.

An overemphasis on cultural differences is highlighting the closed system, is preventing rational dialogue and is hence promoting intolerance. Instead emphasis should be expressed on the similarities between cultures and moving towards a common culture of humanity, which is good for tolerance. A common human culture is making progress on many fronts: gradually more and more countries abolish FGM and the death penalty, whilst LGBT rights and gay marriages are increasingly legalised. Care for our own environment, care for the planet's biodiversity and eradication of neglect and abuse for children are goals already supported by billions of people of different cultural background. To achieve these goals a lower fertility rate for all of us is a key prerequisite. Therefore, education for men and women, abolishing polygamy and teenage marriage and full emancipation for women in the developing world need to be implemented as part of our common human culture.

Some future thoughts

Despite a lot of radicalisation and the highly-publicised clash of civilisations, the world is gradually growing together mainly as a result of globalisation and the internet. Yuval Harari[278] mentions that '*in their conflicts and dilemmas, 21st-century Europeans are very different from their early-modern and medieval ancestors, but are increasingly similar to their Chinese and Indian contemporaries*'. He feels that conflicts will not be between alien civilisations but that we will likely to be involved in '*a fraternal struggle within a single civilisation*'. More relevant modern issues such as global climate change, the pace of biotechnology and ongoing mechanisation of human jobs will be the new arguments and conflicts.

History has taught us that with less people around, unemployment will reduce, just as peasants and serfs gained more bargaining power at the end of the Black Death. This could reduce

[278] https://www.theguardian.com/books/2016/sep/09/isis-global-civilisation-google-yuval-noah-harari

inequality. However, Yuval Harari in his book *Homo Deus*[279] paints a more dystopian picture with ever increasing inequality because of rapid developments of biotechnology, only available for the lucky elites, as well as leaving loads of people out of work due to fast-progressing mechanisation. He asks himself:

"What would the Indian, Brazilian or Nigerian elites prefer? Invest in fixing the problem of hundreds of millions of poor or in upgrading a few million rich? Unlike in the 20th century, when the elite had a stake in fixing the problems of the poor because they were militarily and economically vital, in the 21st century the most efficient (albeit it ruthless) strategy may be to let go of the useless third-class carriages and dash forward with the first class only. In order to compete with Japan, Brazil might need a handful of upgraded super humans far more than millions of healthy ordinary workers."[280]

This may seem cynical and cold, but the majority of the elites have no track record of being social or warm.

The potential for another species (Homo Deus) in the nearby future is real. Harari talks about overcoming immortality, merging with artificial intelligence and creating super-humans or something which is no longer human. This future species might do completely away with Homo sapiens, just as we have exterminated the Neanderthals. This future looks grim, unfair and dangerous for the human race, but not at all unlikely. Harari ends his book with a number of philosophical questions and the last two I am repeating here:[281]

- *What is more valuable – Intelligence or Consciousness?*
- *What will happen to society, politics and daily life when non-conscious but highly intelligent algorithms know us better than we know ourselves?*

---

[279] *Homo Deus: A Brief History of Tomorrow*, Yuval Harari (2016), Harvill Seeker.
[280] Ibid. p.349
[281] Ibid. p.397

Extermination of 'useless humans' is something no one would want. It is true that new developments and evolutionary pressures cannot be stopped. But inclusion of as many people as possible into this unpredictable but exiting future seems more morally justified than dumping *useless third-class carriages*. Unfortunately, biology teaches us that speciation starts from a small specialised or isolated population. But should we meekly follow biological principles? Why not conscientiously reduce the future population so that we all fit in this first-class carriage? We are at the crossroads of changes and we can still influence the fact that a small part of us is running very fast and likes to 'upgrade' themselves into super-humans. We urgently need legislation on genetic manipulation (GM) and artificial intelligence. GM of the human race should not be limited to the lucky few of a rich elite. However, it is already ongoing in the western world, with or without legislation: children are born from three parents[282] and reliable non-invasive screening for Down's syndrome in unborn foetuses will cause a reduction of children born with Down's syndrome, because most mothers will opt for an abortion.[283]

Increased longevity, even without reaching immortality, will put more strain on the world's limited resources and biodiversity. Smaller families are a way to offset population growth, originating from longer lifetimes. Exploding populations will mean poorer living conditions for all of us and will increase the risk for an elite to leave all of us far behind by 'upgrading' into super-humans, with or without artificial intelligence.

Another concern is that we only started to live an urban life during the last hundreds of years. Currently about 54% of the world population lives in cities and that is expected to rise to more than 65% by 2050 (see Figure 10-3). Although we are an adaptable species, we are not really designed to live that close together. We need individual space and privacy and that seems to be ever reducing in big cities. Most people in cities in the developing world live in slums under often abominable

[282] http://www.telegraph.co.uk/news/2016/09/27/worlds-first-baby-born-with-three-parent-baby-technique/
[283] https://www.theguardian.com/commentisfree/2016/oct/06/sally-phillips-woman-unborn-baby-downs-terminate-pregnancy

circumstances, whilst the average apartment size in European cities gets smaller and smaller. Traffic and neighbourhood noise, cooking smells and light pollution only seem to increase. Due to the sheer masses of people and their traffic, laws and regulations are needed. The number of laws and regulations have increased even further in densely populated countries to ease anger and irritation and to create an orderly behaviour within cities. Not only will the flux to cities continue (see Figure 10-3), by 2100 the planet will contain at least another three billion extra people and most of those will live in ever expanding cities.[284]

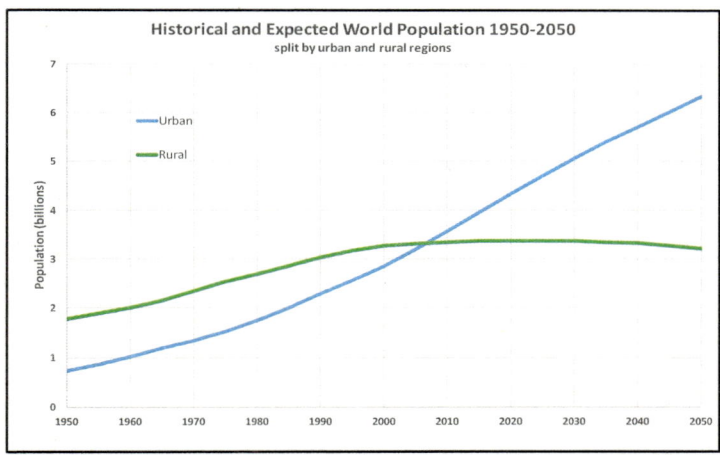

Figure 10-3: Global Urban/rural trends over 1950–2050.[285]

Cities evolve and become very complex. But complexity is also increasing vulnerability. Electricity and water supply become easy targets when cities are under siege during war with horrendous suffering as observed in the Syria (Aleppo) and Iraq

[284] *Adventures in the Anthropocene* by Gaia Vince (2014) Vintage Books. pp 338-381.
[285] United Nations, Department of Economic and Social Affairs, Population Division (2014). World Urbanization Prospects: The 2014 Revision, CD-ROM Edition

(Mosul) wars.[286] Food and living supplies enter a city with a daily traffic of trucks and vans, not only clogging up the arteries but also deteriorating the air quality. Terrorist attacks and natural disasters both have the potential of an elevated number of casualties and misery in densely populated areas. Is there a safe limit to urban size and complexity?

And how far can we go? Do we have an unbounded appetite for tolerance creep? What to do, when slum fights break out due to overcrowding? Or are city-dwellers modifying into a new species, 'Homo Urbanus'? Very adapt to city life, fast, well-behaved, well spoken, without private transportation but completely out of touch with the countryside or with nature. And how would city life be for those billions? Although not a perfect existence either, hunter-gatherers worked a lot less than factory workers[287] and life in nature seems a lot more relaxing than a grim city existence.

A last thought about the future is the principle of a self-regulating planet. In 1979 Jim Lovelock wrote a book *Gaia*,[288] with had a profound influence on people. His idea is that life on the planet functions as a single organism, which defines and maintains its conditions, necessary for survival. The planet is trying to stay in balance by a number of physical and chemical mechanisms (e.g. the balance between the CO_2 in the atmosphere and the oceans). But in the Anthropocene, things are getting out of balance by the much-increased fossil fuel use and population numbers. Altered weather patterns, creating havoc as killer hurricanes (see Figure 10-4) and an increase in sea levels, can they be a sign of the planet metaphorically fighting back? In other words, does the planet possess a negative feedback loop, which is trying to keep the global temperatures under control? Where are the limits and what can be reversed? We know preciously little

[286]http://www.npr.org/sections/thetwo-way/2016/08/09/489296670/2-million-residents-of-war-ravaged-aleppo-now-without-running-water
[287] *Homo Deus: A Brief History of Tomorrow* by Yuval Harari (2016), Harvill Seeker. pp. 175-176
[288] *Gaia* by James Lovelock (1987 version). Oxford University Press.

about the limits of the planet, despite some vague claims on the subject.[289]

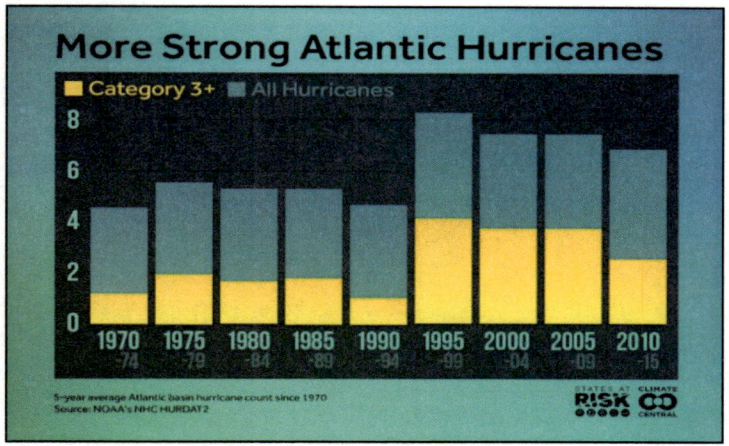

Figure 10-4: Since 1995 there is a marked increase in hurricane intensity occurring in the North Atlantic Ocean Basin.[290]

Similarly, one can argue that fertility rate is being self-regulated by economic circumstances. Raising children costs too much, since the overall cost of living has increased significantly. Living in relative luxury has its price and drives the recent drop in fertility rate in the developed world. Due to low use in contraceptives and cultural bias towards larger families, the fertility rate is not self-regulating in Africa and some Asian countries (e.g. Afghanistan). Instead migration from overpopulated areas is used as an important safety valve[291] whilst food aid is supplied on a regular basis to combat droughts.[292] But

---

[289] *The God Species* by Mark Lynas (2011). Fourth Estate books.

[290] http://www.climatecentral.org/news/atlantic-hurricane-season-major-storms-20682

[291] For how much longer? Walls and fences are increasingly erected in Southern Europe and USA.

[292] There is some moral obligation to help, since droughts caused by climate change are inflicted on the total planet, whilst climate change is disproportionally caused by rich developed countries.

not all problems of the developing world can be blamed on historical colonialism or ongoing exploitations by multi-national corporations. Almost all former colonies are now independent countries for some time. Unfortunately, most of them are ruled by corrupt and/or ruthless regimes. This stifles self-determination for most of the people in the developing countries. They deserve our help to throw off the yoke of corrupt rulers.

Chapter 11
Past and Present Directions on Overpopulation

Limits to Food and Resources

Overpopulation was not an issue before the Industrial Revolution. Diseases, famines and wars kept the population in check. In the 14th century the Black Death even reduced the world population significantly from 450 million to 350–375 million.[293] The concern about overpopulation is however not new. Malthus in his book *The Essay on the Principle of Population*, issued in 1798 was the first of its kind. He used simplistic formulae such as exponentially growing populations combined with an arithmetical growing food supply, which was of course on track of causing trouble. Malthus was a proponent that men should refrain from '*pursuing the dictate of nature in an early attachment to one woman*'. In other words, men should '*marry later in life than had been usual and only at a stage when fully capable of supporting a family*'.[294]

Malthus' view is remarkably prophetic, since later marriages started to occur some 200 years later and economic constraints form the major barrier to large families these days. Malthus was strongly opposed to birth control within marriage however, which proved him completely wrong 200 years later. The arithmetical increase of food also proved a completely wrong assumption, due to his oversight of technological improvements. It should be noted

---

[293] *The Great Leveller* by Walter Scheidel, pp 291-313. Princeton University Press (2017)

[294]http://cgge.aag.org/PopulationandNaturalResources1e/CF_PopNatRes_Jan10/CF_PopNatRes_Jan108.html

however that Malthus lived in a period of relative equilibrium between the population and the agricultural carrying capacity of the planet. The drastic changes in energy availability, medical discoveries and industrial use of fertiliser only occurred much later. The blame and ridicule seem too easy with the benefit of hindsight.

Paul Ehrlich's book *The Population Bomb* (1968) was written without the knowledge of the effects of industrial scale of fertiliser use. He described the pernicious state of the environment and the expected critical food supply. He predicted that in the 1970s hundreds of millions of people would die from starvation. It is now considered an alarmist neo-Malthusian book and its predictions proved to be too pessimistic. Just like Malthus did not foresee the effects of the Industrial Revolution and the concurrent advances in medicines, Ehrlich did not foresee all the beneficial effects of the Green Revolution. Predicting the effects of future technologies is not easy. Quite ahead of his time, Ehrlich suggested a tax scheme in which additional children would add to a family's tax burden at increasing rates for more children. He was also in favour of legalised abortions, the use of mass sterilising agents and using incentives for men to agree on vasectomies.[295] With respect to food aid, his opinion was very harsh, since he would only provide food aid to countries, who have an ability to become self-sufficient on food in the future. But he does not describe how to judge that ability and how far in the future he would be prepared to look.

Ehrlich's book was a best-seller and has definitely influenced the other famous book of that era *Limits to Growth*,[296] also known as the report for the Club of Rome in 1972. This was the first book addressing sustainability and sold more than 30 million copies. For the first time, computers were used to predict population growth, reserves for oil, coal and ore and estimates of pollution. Although reserves for resources were significantly underestimated, the report predicted the world population very

---

[295] *The Population Bomb* by Paul R. Ehrlich, pp. 165–66. Ballantine Books (1968).
[296] *The Limits to Growth* – A report for the Club of Rome Project on the Predicament of Mankind. Dennis L. Meadows ea. (1972)

accurately. The report is not giving any solutions; it only highlights potential clashes between supply and demand. When I first read the book, the pictures of our fragile blue planet taken by Apollo astronauts, came to my mind. It is the first time I got a concept of limits and that the earth is a finite place. Despite the flaws in the assumptions for the predictions, the awakening sense of planetary boundaries is probably the best thing about this book.

Amongst other literature on the subject, the book *Limits to Growth* inspired a top Chinese official, called Song Jian, during a visit to Europe in 1979. The Chinese communist party leaders, headed by Deng Xiaoping, subsequently started to implement the infamous one-child policy in China between 1978 and 1980. Unfortunately, implementation did not come that easy and the policy was enforced by fines, pressure for abortions and even forced sterilisations. The policy was not all-encompassing in the country and has always been restricted to Han Chinese, living in urban areas, where overpopulation was a major concern. It is estimated that the one-child policy has reduced the Chinese population by as much as 300 million over its first 20 years.[297] Despite these harsh measures and controversy outside China, 76% of the Chinese people approved of the one-child policy in a 2008 independent survey.[298] The one-child policy has been formally phased out as of 2015, when it became officially a two-child policy.[299]

Population control has not been limited to China. Indira Gandhi in the early 1970s introduced a compulsory sterilisation programme for men with two children or more. The programme failed, because many unmarried young men, political opponents and ignorant, poor men were sterilised.[300] These forced sterilisations created a public aversion to family planning, which was long remembered afterwards. Therefore, recent family planning efforts in India are focussed on women. Forceful family planning creates a bad name and can linger a long time and is thus

---

[297]http://geography.about.com/od/populationgeography/a/onechild.htm
[298]http://www.pewglobal.org/2008/07/22/the-chinese-celebrate-their-roaring-economy-as-they-struggle-with-its-costs/
[299] http://www.bbc.co.uk/news/world-asia-34665539
[300]http://www.bbc.co.uk/news/world-asia-india-30040790

causing adverse effects on what was planned in the first place. Lessons should be learned on this negative experiment on Indian men, and similar experiments on African men should be strictly forbidden.

Environmental Impact

Historical considerations of overpopulation were so far focussed on the immediate repercussions on the human population itself, such as food security and resource availability. Gradually people starting to think about wider implications such as the biodiversity and sustainability of the planet. Concepts such as environmental impact, carrying capacity and ecological (or carbon) footprint became commonly known. On environmental impact, Paul Ehrlich together with John Holdren and Barry Commoner[301] developed an idea on the main factors influencing the impact on the environment. Their findings became known as the I = PAT equation, in which:

I = environmental **I**mpact

P = human **P**opulation

A = human **A**ffluence

T = the Resource Intensity or **T**echnology

Since the Population (P), Affluence (A) and Technology (T) have different environmental impacts, are highly non-linear in character and cause dependencies, the equation should be written more general as a function of three (dependent) variables:

$$I = f(P, A, T)$$

The impact of the Resource Intensity (T) can increase the environmental impact but also reduce it. Also, the total environmental impact is the summation of the environmental impact of each individual human being, rather than the product of the total world Population and average world Affluence:

---

[301] Impact of Population Growth by Paul R. Ehrlich and John P. Holdren (1971). American Association for the Advancement of Science **171** (3977): 1212–1217

$$I = \Sigma \, f \, (P_i * A_i * T_i)$$

For example, an American going to the shop by car in an SUV has a much bigger environmental impact (A*T) than an African doing his/her shopping on foot. Affluence and the Technology used can make a massive difference.

Several NGOs have realised that there are limits to growth and impact on the planet. Here are a few quotes to illustrate this:

"If 9 billion people aspired to live at the level of affluence achieved in the OECD nations, the global economy would need to be 15 times the size of this one by 2050 and 40 times bigger by the end of the century."[302]

"At present, there are no well-charted ways for 10 billion people to achieve lifestyles like those enjoyed in the Most Developed Countries, because the only known way forward is economic growth, and that will come into collision with the finite earth. Technology can help, but without socio-political change it cannot solve. There is much work to be done."[303]

One cannot have it all on a finite planet and to illustrate the boundaries of the three main variables: Population, Affluence and Planetary Wellbeing (as a proxy to positive Environmental Impact) a limiting surface[304] can be defined in a 3D space (see Figure 11-1). This sketch suggests that we can only exist within the bounded volume. However, we are currently living beyond our means and have moved from a sustainable position inside the bounded volume (black point in Figure 11-2) to a position on the blue boundary surface (red point in Figure 11-2) over the course of the last 200 years. We cannot go outside this bounded volume, so any future path has its trajectory along the boundary surface (blue arrows in Figure 11-2). So, there are choices to make: what

---

[302]http://www.populationmatters.org/documents/cpre_report.pdf

[303]https://royalsociety.org/~/media/Royal_Society_Content/policy/projects/people-planet/2012-04-25-PeoplePlanet.pdf p. 98

[304] The surface has been depicted flat for simplicity purposes. It is very likely to be curved and potentially irregular.

we currently do is to maintain (or even increase) our human affluence per capita and increase the population at the dramatic cost to the planetary wellbeing (path B): we are living beyond our means. Alternative paths to cope with a similar or increasing population are path A (same population, increased planetary wellbeing but dramatic loss in human affluence) or path C (maintain the planet's wellbeing, limited population growth and reduced human affluence).

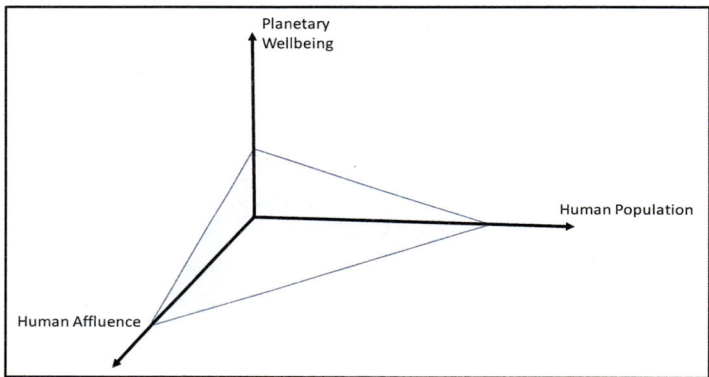

Figure 11-1: The bounded surface of our finite planet: we cannot have it all

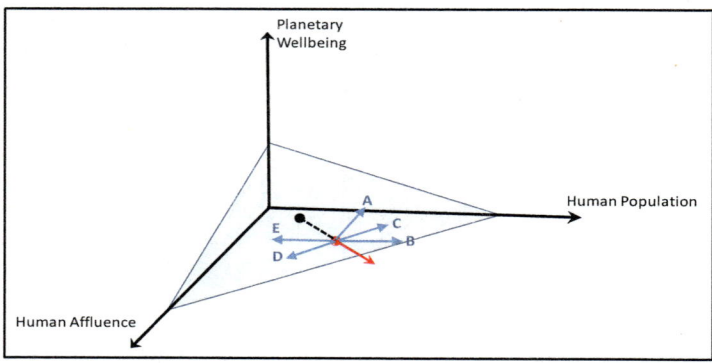

Figure 11-2: We are at the moment on the boundary surface and have choices to make

More appropriate paths along the boundary surface of Figure 11-2 would be to reduce the population: path D by maintaining the planet's wellbeing at current levels whilst increasing the human affluence or by path E, whereby the planet's wellbeing is increased, whilst the affluence is only modestly increased. But better still rather than balancing along the boundary surface, would be to position ourselves within the bounded volume.

Figures 11-1 and 11-2 limit themselves to the current available technology. We have evidence that our innovations can alter the position of this boundary surface dramatically. As an example, the effects of the Industrial and Green Revolutions on the boundary surface are shown in Figure 11-3 as a new (pink) boundary surface.

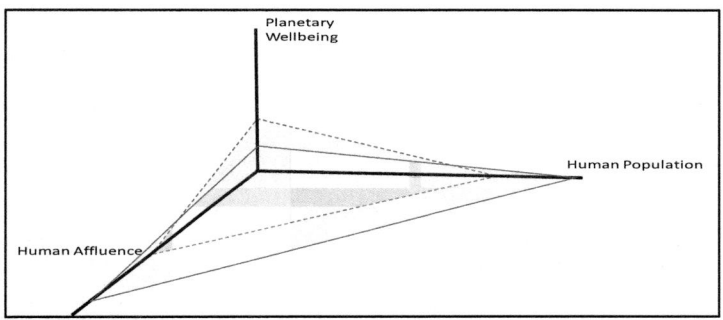

Figure 11-3: The massive use of Fossil Fuels (Industrial Revolution) or Fertilisers (Green Revolution) enabled a large increase in Human Population and Affluence but at the dramatic cost of the Planetary Wellbeing (pink versus original blue boundary surface)

But new technologies do not always have a negative effect on the planet's wellbeing: the introduction of large scale genetically modified (GM) crops, could in theory reduce the amount of fertiliser or pesticide use,[305] but could also reduce biodiversity. Figure 11-4 has assumed a neutral effect on the environment, allowing the population to expand due to the introduction of GM

---

[305] The effect can be currently debated, but future developments may go in that direction.

crops. I have left the Affluence axis unaltered, because that is what is probably happening.

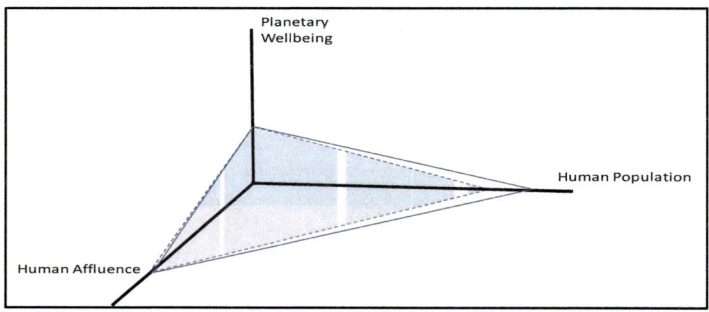

Figure 11-4: The effect of the introduction of GM-crops on the boundary surface. The planetary wellbeing is assumed to be constant. The population can rise because of this, but overall human affluence is constant or very marginally increasing. The increasing population will likely have an additional downward pressure on the planetary wellbeing (not depicted).

As a last example of the influence of technology, I have used the example of replacing fossil fuel-based energy by renewable energy (Figure 11-5), to illustrate that this could improve the planet's wellbeing significantly (reduction of greenhouse gasses). This form of technological change could allow the population to increase, whilst keeping the human affluence (and implicitly the inequality) similar. Alternatively, this changed boundary surface could also be tilted by increasing affluence, whilst keeping the population the same.

Although the interdependencies are realised in the literature, articles are focussed mostly on the western world. The impact to reduce the fertility rate in the west even further is very important because our 'Affluence' is so much bigger and our 'Technology' so much more wasteful than in the developing world. But for both the developed as the developing world it would be better to '*make people happy'*, to quote Travis Rieder,[306] rather than *'happily making people'*.[307] In other words, we should focus our technologies to improve our average 'Affluence' by lifting billions out of poverty, rather than increasing the world's population (unlike the new boundary surfaces in Figures 11-4 and 11-5).

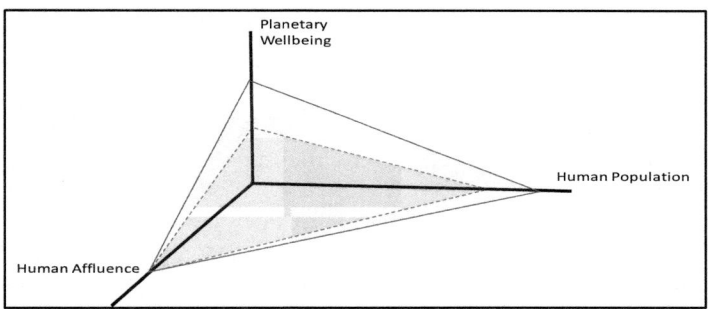

Figure 11-5: The effect of replacing fossil fuel-based energy by renewables on the boundary surface. The planetary wellbeing is increasing due to a drop of CO_2 levels (on the long run, however). Population can increase at a constant affluence. Note that the increasing population will likely have an additional downward pressure on the planetary wellbeing (not depicted).

It is not just the Environment

Since no one foresees serious limits to food production or resources in the immediate future, the current focus of overpopulation is biased towards the environmental impact. The other side of the overpopulation coin (large families perpetuate poverty, neglect and migration) does not feature enough in the

---

[306]https://www.theguardian.com/commentisfree/2016/sep/12/why-we-should-have-fewer-children-save-the-planet-climate-change#comment-83154506
[307] I changed Rieder's *"making happy people"* into *"happily making people"*, since the act of procreation is generally a happy event. Many extra people in this world will not have a happy life, since they will mostly end up in the poorest decile, so *"making happy people"* seems unlikely.

debate on overpopulation. In 2010, the organisation 'Save the Children' quoted:

"Given its detrimental impacts on poverty reduction, it is surprising that the issue of population growth has received so little attention over the last decade from development donors, agencies and developing countries alike."[308]

The United Nations Population Fund and the World Health Organisation (WHO) are actively pursuing the use of contraception amongst other goals, such as gender equality and eradicating female genital mutilation (FGM). Although contraceptive use is on the rise, over 200 million women worldwide would like to avoid a pregnancy but are not using an effective method of contraception. The reasons vary for each country but are related to a lack of supplies, cultural and political barriers and poor quality of services.[309]

Apart from 'Save the Children', several other NGOs such as 'Population Matters',[310] 'Marie Stopes International'[311] and the 'Gates Foundation'[312] are actively promoting contraception and indirectly emancipation of women. This is all on a voluntary basis, but it is noted that they are working against a strong pro-birth culture, which requires able communication efforts. One of the big challenges deserving focus is the elimination of teenage pregnancies in the developing world. This can be addressed by making contraceptives readily available, by education of young women but most important of all by changing a culture (see below).

Eliminating teenage pregnancies works positively in many ways: firstly, less young women will die of childbirth since teenagers are twice as likely to die from complications in

---

[308]https://www.savethechildren.org.uk/sites/default/files/docs/Population_p olicy_briefing_1.pdf

[309] http://www.who.int/reproductivehealth/en/

[310] https://www.populationmatters.org/

[311] https://mariestopes.org/

[312] http://www.gatesfoundation.org/What-We-Do/Global-Development/ Family- Planning

pregnancy as are women in their twenties.[313] Secondly, children born to teenage mothers receive less care due to inexperience of the mother (or father). Thirdly, teenage girls and women have a right to develop themselves: raising children is hard work and can hardly be combined with work or studying. Fourthly, the fertility rate will drop when first pregnancies are delayed.

It needs to be addressed by NGOs concerned about children's health that raising large families is detrimental for all children. By moving from the countryside to cities, away from traditional extended families, large families can hardly flourish. In the developed world, carers and childminders, who are responsible for larger groups of children, require years of study before they can work. Rearing a large family is a very serious business and it should be ensured that parents are capable to do this. NGOs concerned about children's health should actively discourage large families.

Apart from the negative effects of large families or early pregnancies, the economic consequences of overpopulation need to be better estimated. Having too many people is not a blessing for an economy: due to progressive mechanisation, the number of available meaningful jobs will be limited if not reduce, causing an increase in unemployment or, at best, subsistence jobs. Overpopulation in cities is causing choking congestion, poor air quality and consequent massive economic losses. The fear of an aging population and absence of support in old age has proven wrong in many countries with a declining population. Besides, this is only a temporary demographic bulge, which will disappear over time when the population stabilises to sustainable levels.

Children in the Developed World: Only for the Rich and Smart?

Racist and supremacist solutions often reverted to genocide or eugenics to make space for a preferred group of people in a country. The Armenian genocide, in which the Turks of the

---

[313]http://www.independent.co.uk/news/world/africa/when-teenage-pregnancy-is-a-death-sentence-7878743.html

Ottoman Empire killed 75% of the Armenian population[314], between 1915 and 1923 is one example. The Nazis in Germany used similar ideas to exterminate Jews in the Second World War. Jews and Armenians were a diversity threat for these countries and there was no place for different ethnicities or religions. But also, gypsies and homosexuals were prosecuted in Nazi Germany, because they were seen as respectively less racially pure or deviant. Eugenics not only took off in Nazi Germany but also in the US: compulsory sterilisations and forced euthanasia (which is murder) of mentally and physically disabled as well as people with a low IQ took place under the cover of legislation. As late as 1972 it was found that 2000 involuntary sterilisations had been carried out in the US on poor black welfare mothers with multiple children.[315]

Under the influence of science and the horrors of exterminations in Germany, eugenics in the US gradually waned. But even in the 1980s, Singapore adopted an active promotion of larger families for the better educated, whilst offering cash incentives for the lower classes to be sterilised.[316] Fortunately, this only lasted till 1987. In the 21st century eugenics is not dead however, it comes under a different disguise as a means to eradicate diseases or to prevent disabled children.

A small step towards eugenics is only to allow children when you can afford it. The economic situation is already forcing a lot of people in Europe, America and Asia to have small families voluntarily. Similarly, there is a tendency in the developed world to admire large families for the rich and smart. Large families start to become the domain of celebrity chefs (Jamie Oliver, Gordon Ramsey), rich politicians (Tony Blair, Boris Johnson) or philandering pop stars (Mick Jagger, Rod Stewart, Paul Weller). A large trophy family seems one of the ways to show-off your wealth as a status symbol. The gutter press only seems to rub this in with glamorous family photos thus giving a very poor example

---

[314] http://www.theblaze.com/stories/2013/04/25/the-1915-armenian-genocide-why-is-it-still-denied-by-turkey-and-the-u-s/
[315] *Poor Women, Powerful Men: America's Great Experiment in Family Planning* by Martha C. Ward. Westview Press (1986) p. 95.
[316] *Peoplequake*. Fred Pearce (2011) Eden Project Books, p.155.

to less well-off couples. This large family behaviour seems to tap into old stereotypical patriarchal patterns of big powerful leaders, having sired hundreds or thousands of children (e.g. Genghis Khan). Behaviour like this is no longer of this age and is detrimental for the emancipation of women. It should be shamed and blamed rather than glorified by the media.

Showing off with large families is not limited to the developed world. It is probably even more prevalent in the developing world: polygamous South-African president Jacob Zuma has 20 children and Nigerian President Mohammadu Buhari has 10 children. But if we tolerate and glorify large families for the rich and smart elites in the developed world, it is hypocritical to point fingers to the developing world.

Parenting in the Developing World: Education and Cultural Change

Compared to men, women are less educated in the developing world and consequently less equal. Education in the developing countries should therefore be more focussed on educating women, who need an indispensable catch up. Although sexual education and family planning is also focussed on women, this focus is mainly on post-natal care and hygiene for infants, which is useful in countries with tropical diseases. What lacks in their education is how to deal with older children, how to deal with conflict between children (e.g. bullying), how to provide examples as parents and how to protect children from neglect or abuse. The quality of child-rearing is worth highlighting since only with more involved parents, children stand a chance to fully develop, to be less abused or neglected and, hopefully, to get out of a poverty trap. Logically family size need to be discussed when educating young parents.

It is generally accepted that the most important need for change in the developing countries, is education. Compulsory secondary education for both boys and girls will delay teenage marriage and pregnancies. Even more important in patriarchal societies is to educate the men on gender equality, sustainability and poverty traps. It is predominantly men who prolong antiquated patriarchy, under the protective umbrella of 'culture'.

We need to have frank conversations with men who want large families (men normally want more children than women in the developing world): what is the point creating large families, if one's children die of hunger, have no work and are forced to migrate to support the large family? What pride does a father see in that? Why are poor families in the developed world and China restraining themselves and have small families, but even poorer sub-Saharan families are not? The main causes are patriarchy and related polygyny and these are the causes which need to be eliminated. Contraception only works if one embraces common sense and abandons the stranglehold of narrow thinking, fed for centuries by ancient cultures. Self-determination is not looking back to long-gone cultures, but looking forward.

More focus is needed on a common human culture, rather than emphasising cultural differences. Cultures are not forever and cannot form the basis for an entitlement. The law of a country always goes above cultures. Stricter law enforcements are needed to stamp out excesses such as honour killings, which is fortunately happening.[317] Rational dialogue among individuals of different groups is precluded, since each group has its own truth and standards for its attainment.[318] Emphasising one's culture can be anti-individualistic, does not promote thinking and can be divisive.

After China and India last century, there have been several countries successfully curbing their population growth. Iran,[319] Singapore and Algeria have all managed to reduce their fertility rates by education, making contraceptives readily available and raising awareness by other means. However, in Iran, an apparent U-turn is in the making, since the religious leadership fears an aging population and has slammed family planning as an imitation of western lifestyle.[320] A law is now banning vasectomies and

[317]https://www.theguardian.com/world/2016/oct/06/pakistan-honor-killing-law-prison-sentence
[318] http://www.quebecoislibre.org/010804-13.htm
[319] http://www.un.org/esa/population/publications /completingfertility/2 RevisedABBASIpaper.PDF
[320] https://www.theguardian.com/world/2015/mar/11/iran-ban-voluntary-sterilisation-contraceptive-access-block-boost-population

cutting access to contraceptives. It remains to be seen whether Iran's population, that enjoyed access to family planning for more than 20 years, will abide.

Sarah Harper mentions that the demographic change caused by reducing fertility is not solely a function of increasing affluence, as many economists think. The reality is that demographic change also depends on political and democratic change and overcoming socio-cultural differences.[321] She also highlights that the complex interplays between demographic change, economic change and socio-political change are bi-directional (e.g. GDP increase causes a fertility drop and vice versa). There are success stories in South-East Asia and to a lesser extent in Latin America. However, the Middle East and Africa are lagging and she fears that these regions are maybe not enough developed to drive a much-needed demographic change. And reversely she argues that *age-structural change is as important to a country's development as economic and political change*.[322]

In a highly-connected world, there is no more place for massive gender inequality. The Nigerian President, Mohammadu Buhari, deserved ridicule, when he stated in Europe that his wife, who critiqued his leadership, *'belongs in his kitchen'* and subsequently claimed *'superior knowledge'*.[323] These things can no longer be said in the developed world and people better get used to it. Gender equality is one of the big drivers for smaller families and should be promoted even before discussing family planning. Again, this boils down to frank conversations with men. Without an attitudinal change in men, gender equality is bound to fail.

Sustainability in the Developing World

We cannot immediately demand overall sustainability from poor developing countries. Western countries took so much away during slavery times and colonisation and even now modern

---

[321] *How Population Change Will Transform Our World.* Sarah Harper (2016) Oxford University Press, p. 171

[322] Ibid p. 173

[323]https://www.theguardian.com/world/2016/oct/14/nigerias-president-says-wife-belongs-to-my-kitchen

corporations with the help of local corrupt leaders continue to strip valuable forests, minerals, oil and gas from the developing world to sell them at a good profit in the developed countries. Historian David Olusoga[324] claims that the slave traders and the colonial past are barely acknowledged. First of all, it is about truth which is hard to find in whitewashed skewed history books, in which the enslavers and colonisers were always the heroes and never the bad guys. For example, Britain's role as slave trader, slave owner and coloniser has never been apologised towards black nations. Only after a formal apology, one can start the process of reconciliation. Slave trading/owning and colonising nations have often accumulated their wealth from the days of slavery[325] or by plundering resources from colonies.[326] Colonies were often left in poverty and stripped off most of its assets at the time when independence was granted or fought over.

Without a redistribution of wealth, it is not moral to demand sustainability from developing nations. The poorest nations deserve our financial help to educate girls and women so that they can fully develop and marriages are delayed; to educate boys and men on out of date patriarchal and preconceived ideas, such as polygyny and big families, so that fertility rates will drop. In the western world, we managed to create a safety net for old age in the form of pensions and affordable healthcare, partly based on the wealth our nations accumulated during a slave trading/owning and colonial past. The creation of a social security system for the old and ill in poor developing nations is therefore a moral obligation. This creation of a safety net for the old and ill is the best investment of future reparation payments. And, a proper safety net for old age and illness will reduce the urge to create a large family for one's future care and consequently reduce the fertility rate.

---

[324]https://www.theguardian.com/books/2016/nov/04/david-olusoga-interview-black-history

[325]http://www.independent.co.uk/news/uk/home-news/the-stately-homes-built-on-the-back-of-slaves-8518002.html

[326] Only the silver originating from the Americas over 300 years is worth more than $500 trillion at today's silver prices, see *The Spanish Treasure Fleets* by Timothy R. Walton (1994)

Advertise, Inform and Mass Media

In the past, family planning has progressed a lot by advertisements of small and happy families. With success, both Iran and Singapore (see Figure 11-6) have actively advertised family planning in public. In Iran family planning was advertised everywhere: in bus stops, public spaces, parks, cinemas, and even on children's toys and chocolate boxes.

Media have a big role to play: there is strong empirical evidence that role models influence behaviour. Population-value-based drama series on television in Mexico and India and radio programmes in Kenia and Tanzania indicated significant shifts in beliefs about the acceptability and practicality of family planning and ideal family size.[327] This in turn has led in many cases to increased use of family planning and reduced or delayed childbearing. The same reference (327) quotes William Ryerson in saying that '*in terms of births averted per dollar spent mass media communications are probably the most effective strategy for reducing fertility rates*'.

The importance of role models and celebrity endorsement should not be underestimated. It is known from the advertising world, that this is a formula, which works for almost anything. For the same reason, it is counter-productive for the promotion of small families to show rich celebrity chefs, politicians or pop-stars with their numerous offspring on television or in the gutter press. Instead, these types of show-offs should be ridiculed, shamed and blamed. The media have therefore an important ethical role in this to play and it is important to bring them on board about population reduction. To have more than two children should be frowned upon.

Some of these mass media and celebrity endorsements of smaller families could be interpreted as psychological manipulation. But this is as much manipulation as the tax-breaks and transport fare-reductions for large families. It can therefore be viewed as a counterbalance for the promotion of large families. I see the promotion of smaller families on posters, billboards, television and by celebrities in the same light as the promotions to

---

[327]http://www.npr.org/documents/2016/jun/population_engineering.pdf

stop smoking or to eat less sugar. Smaller families are good for your health, for the health of your children, for the health of the environment and for the health of the economy.

Figure 11-6: A historical Family Planning Poster from Singapore in the 1970s

Stimulus or Coercion?

Choice enhancing interventions[327] such as education and improved health care access historically have taken decades to impact fertility rate substantially. Preference adjustment measures, such as advertisements and celebrity endorsements may be counteracted by rich or religious promoters of large families. So, is it time to use positive and negative incentives to steer the size of the population?

One of the immediate logical actions would be to abolish promotions for large families, such as child benefits, tax breaks related to family size or transport reductions for large families. However, this would disproportionately harm the poorest of us all. Various measures are already in place to curb child benefit for high income earners: in the UK, there exists a high-income child benefit charge and similar income dependencies exist elsewhere.

In the UK, child benefit is higher for the first child and is lower but constant for every additional child (around two thirds of the first child's benefit).

Only the most affluent countries in the world have a child benefit system, but currently there are no countries which have a child benefit cap for the number of children. On the contrary, there are several countries, which are actively stimulating large families, such as Belgium (see Figure 11-7). Child benefit is roughly proportional with the number of children in Scandinavia, the Netherlands and the US. Both France and Germany stimulate larger families, but less so than Belgium. Strange enough, France does not support one child families with child benefit, and benefits only start at the second child. Only the UK has a regressive policy by giving less money per child for the second and following children. Developed countries are primarily responsible for climate change and loss of biodiversity. Reducing the population in developed countries should be encouraged. Child benefit should only be paid to the very poorest of us and stop after two children.

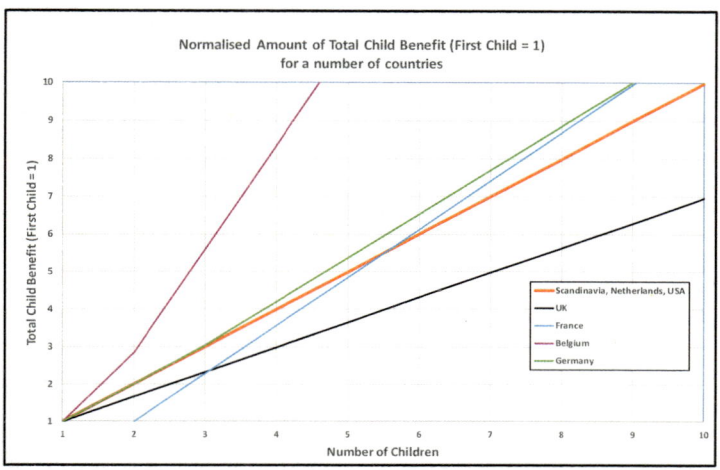

Figure 11-7: Normalised (one child=1) child benefit as a function of family size: there is no real discouragement for large families in most countries (based on data available in 2016).

Since child benefit is a relatively small amount, probably more discouragement is needed than only abolishing this. This could be done by introducing a child-tax for families of more than two children, progressive with the number of children and severely progressive with income to prevent that the rich elites still can afford large families. This should be taxed on the income of each parent. It is realised that this may cause some heart-breaking situations, when divorced couples with children from a previous relationship have a wish to form a new family. One must draw a line somewhere however since there is a trade-off between justice on a microscopic scale versus justice on macroscopic national or global scale. Introduction of a child-tax will hopefully also work as a deterrent to think twice to have children with a partner: a poor or mediocre relationship does not get better by raising children together. On the contrary a lot of relationships fail, when under stress from parenthood.

Cash incentives may help to promote family planning training for adolescents and young adults to prepare them for the responsibilities and financial consequences of raising children. Family planning and parental training should become an obligatory subject in secondary schooling. Cash incentives for sterilisation or vasectomy could work as well, albeit only in combination with an income progressive child-tax, else this will only target the poorer people. Coercive sterilisations, vasectomy or abortions should never be promoted, since it invades the right to decide what happens with one's own body.

I understand Sarah Corly's plea[328] to allow couples in the developed world only one child: one child gives enough parental experience to satisfy the desire of most human beings; one child per couple will reduce the population of the developed world faster, which is much needed to combat an unsustainable destruction of the environment. Again, one can only tackle sustainability of the developing world by showing that we can live sustainably in the developed world, without taking excessively from other parts of the world.

---

[328] *One Child, Do We Have a Right to More?* Sarah Corly (2016) Oxford University Press

Pragmatically however, I think that we should lay the bar at two children. Above that everybody knows that we are increasing the population, which is not very ethical or social towards others. Moreover, I think that a one-child policy is even more difficult to implement and will meet more resistance (see historical evidence from China). Migrants from developing countries used to a high fertility rate, who enter the developed world, have already to adapt tremendously to any limits in family size. Promotion of a two-child policy in developing nations is easier than promoting a one-child policy. Why make different rules for the developing and developed world? The distinction between the two is vague and is a spectrum, rather than a dichotomy. A strict maximum two-child policy should start in the developed world for everybody, including religious people, migrants and refugees, giving off the strongest possible signal: this is the new normal and more than two children is not done. A two-child policy rather than a one-child policy also prevents sliding into a too steep and potentially unstable inversion of the population pyramid.

Temper Life Expectancy

We are transitioning to a smaller and sustainable world population, which will not stress the environment, allow sufficient biodiversity and which has food and water quantities for everybody. In order to regain this paradise, fertility rates need to drop worldwide. But dropping fertility rates will increase the size of the old age cohort during this transition and implicitly increase financial offers of the working age cohort as well as necessitate a delayed pension age.

However, increase in life expectancy is also causing the population to rise. Promoting an unbridled expansion of longevity will only aggravate this. Restraint to reduce the world population should not only be borne by limiting offspring to families. With continuing inequality and without sufficient funds, the old age cohort will suffer more and more. I would suggest channelling money from medical research, aimed to extend life at increasing costs, to social care of the increasing old age cohort to provide a smooth and dignified quality of life in this transition period. Alternatively, other spending choices should be questioned: why spending billions in space research or defence? Should care for the young and old not take priority?

When we have 'regained paradise' in a world without suffering and in harmony with our environment, we can focus on extending life and longevity.